ON THE GODS
AND
OTHER ESSAYS

ON THE GODS
AND
OTHER ESSAYS

ROBERT G.
INGERSOLL
PREFACE BY PAUL KURTZ

PROMETHEUS BOOKS
Buffalo, New York

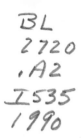

Illustration on full title page
Birthplace of Robert G. Ingersoll
Dresden, N.Y. August 11, 1833

Preface copyright © 1990 Paul Kurtz

Published 1990 by Prometheus Books
700 East Amherst Street, Buffalo, New York 14215

Library of Congress Cataloging-in-Publication Data

Ingersoll, Robert Green, 1833–1899.
    On the gods and other essays / by Robert G. Ingersoll.
        p.   cm.
    Contents: The gods—Thomas Paine—Individuality—Heretics
and heresies—The ghosts.
    ISBN 0-87975-629-2 (alk. paper)
    1. Free thought. I. Title.
BL2720.A2I535   1990
211'.7—dc 20   90-40283
                                                              CIP

Printed on acid-free paper in the United States of America

CONTENTS

"We are indebted solely to science—the only lever capable of raising mankind. Abject faith is barbarism; reason is civilization. To obey is slavish; to act from a sense of obligation perceived by the reason, is noble. Ignorance worships mystery; Reason explains it: the one grovels, the other soars."

—Robert G. Ingersoll
from his essay on "Humboldt"

ACKNOWLEDGMENTS

The publication of this volume is made possible by a grant from Mr. William A. Higgins, who has also done much to help bring about the restoration of the Robert Ingersoll birthplace in Dresden, New York.

PREFACE

Robert Ingersoll: The Great Agnostic

Paul Kurtz

Robert Green Ingersoll was born in Dresden, New York, in 1833. He was the son of John Ingersoll, an itinerant Congregational minister, who, like many others, had been brought to Western New York in the early nineteenth century by the newly opened Erie Canal. Dresden, a small town on Lake Seneca, was a stopping-off place on the journey west between the Hudson River at Albany, at the easternmost point of the canal, and Buffalo on Lake Erie, the westernmost point.

Western New York of the early nineteenth century has been called the "burnt-over district" because of the waves of new settlers brought there from all four corners of the globe. The area became a veritable breeding ground for religious and social movements of every description. Palmyra, New York, was the home of Joseph Smith, and the site of his alleged revelation in 1823 from Moroni (the "angel of the lord"). It was also the place where Smith composed the Book of Mormon. At Hydesville, just east of Rochester, the famous Fox sisters had their first supposed contact with the spirit world in 1848, from which the movement known as spiritualism was born. The Seventh Day Adventists emerged as a religious sect in upstate New York, with the Millerites and Mary Ellen White at their head. Western New York is also the home of the women's rights movement, which had been founded by Elizabeth Cady Stanton in Seneca Falls, New York, not far from where Ingersoll was born.

Ingersoll's birthplace, a handsome white woodframe structure just up the street from his father's church and not far from the lake, has recently been rededicated and restored as a memorial museum and library in his honor. Although the Ingersoll family moved from Dresden shortly after young Robert's birth, the town holds a special place in the hearts of many as the birthplace of a great American and freethinker. Ingersoll's father was himself a stalwart abolitionist, whose views no doubt impressed his son. But Robert was later to reject his religious upbringing to become for many the greatest agnostic of his time. This is especially remarkable given the climate in which Ingersoll had been raised.

Robert Ingersoll was a commanding figure in the nineteenth century. Trained as a lawyer, he practiced in Peoria, Illinois, from 1854 to 1876. During the Civil War Ingersoll became a colonel in the Union Army and was given command of the Eleventh Illinois Cavalry. He moved to Washington, D.C., in 1876, where he devoted his efforts to law and public speaking. Indeed, many people considered Ingersoll to be the greatest orator of his day. An imposing man, full of wit and wisdom, he attracted thousands to his lectures as he traveled from coast to coast.

Ingersoll was elected Attorney General of the State of Illinois shortly after the Civil War—the only elected position he ever held. Yet he became a power in the Republican party, and was considered by many to be its chief publicist. A strong opponent of slavery, Ingersoll supported the election of Abraham Lincoln and all subsequent candidates of the "Grand Old Party." His June 1876 "Plumed Knight" nominating speech for the candidacy of James G. Blaine at the Republican Convention in Cincinnati had a powerful social and political effect (even though Blaine lost the bid for the presidency). It is said that had Ingersoll modified his strong agnostic views and his many attacks on religion, he might have been elected governor of Illinois. His propensity to point out the contradictions of the Bible, to expose the hypocrisy of organized religion, and to defend science and reason made Ingersoll a risky candidate.

Ingersoll was admired as a noble humanitarian, an advocate of human rights, and a defender of unpopular causes—including the rights of the poor, blacks, women, and the dispossessed. Many nineteenth-century intellectual leaders and social activists looked to him for moral authority: Thomas Alva Edison, Mark Twain, Margaret Sanger, Eugene V. Debs, Elizabeth Cady Stanton, Andrew Carnegie, Luther Burbank, Walt Whitman, and others. Robert Ingersoll died on July 21, 1899, in Dobbs Ferry, New York.

In 1901, twelve volumes of Ingersoll's speeches and writings were published in Dresden, New York, and soon became known as the Dresden Edition.

The five selections presented here are taken from the first volume of the Dresden Edition. They express Ingersoll's anti-clericalism and his defense of agnosticism and rationalism. Although Ingersoll was neither a trained philosopher nor a scholar and made few contributions to any field of scholarship, he possessed the uncanny ability to transmit to ordinary people an appreciation for freethought and agnosticism. And for this reason he made a lasting impression on his own generation and the many that followed. Although Robert Ingersoll lived before the development of the Secular Humanist Movement, there is no doubt that he qualifies as one of the great heroes of the Humanist Pantheon.

Unfortunately, all too many people have forgotten America's leading agnostic. To keep alive his memory, the Robert Ingersoll Memorial Committee was founded in 1986 by the Council for Democratic and Secular Humanism. Its purpose is twofold: (1) to preserve Ingersoll's birthplace as a permanent museum and

library, and (2) to keep alive an appreciation for his many contributions to agnosticism and freethought by publishing his views
and making his ideas better known to a public sorely in need
of his enlightened perspective. This volume of Ingersoll's lectures
is dedicated to the latter goal. We hope that, in a modest way,
it will bring to public attention the contributions of a man whose
intellectual legacy lives on almost a century after his death.

THE GODS

THE GODS

AN HONEST GOD IS THE NOBLEST WORK OF MAN

Each nation has created a god, and the god has always resembled his creators. He hated and loved what they hated and loved, and he was invariably found on the side of those in power. Each god was intensely patriotic, and detested all nations but his own. All these gods demanded praise, flattery, and worship. Most of them were pleased with sacrifice, and the smell of innocent blood has ever been considered a divine perfume. All these gods have insisted upon having a vast number of priests, and the priests have always insisted upon being supported by the people, and the principal business of these priests has been to boast about their god, and to insist that he could easily vanquish all the other gods put together.

These gods have been manufactured after numberless models, and according to the most grotesque fashions. Some have a thousand arms, some a hundred heads, some are adorned with necklaces of living snakes, some are armed with clubs, some with sword and shield, some with bucklers, and some have wings as a cherub; some were invisible, some would show themselves entire, and some would only show their backs; some were jealous, some were foolish, some turned themselves into men, some into swans, some into bulls, some into doves, and some into Holy Ghosts, and made love to the beautiful daughters of men. Some were married— all ought to have been—and some were considered as old bachelors from all eternity. Some had children, and the children were turned into gods and worshiped as their fathers had been. Most of these gods were revengeful, savage, lustful, and ignorant. As they generally depended upon their priests for information, their ignorance can hardly excite our astonishment.

These gods did not even know the shape of the worlds they had created, but supposed them perfectly flat. Some thought the day could be lengthened by stopping the sun, that the blowing of horns could throw down the walls of a city, and all knew so little of the real nature of the people they had created, that they commanded the people to love them. Some were so ignorant as to suppose that man could believe just as he might desire, or as they might command, and that to be governed by observation, reason, and experience was a most foul and damning sin. None of these gods could give a true account of the creation of this little earth. All were woefully deficient in geology and astronomy. As a rule, they were most miserable legislators, and as executives, they were far inferior to the average of American presidents.

These deities have demanded the most abject and degrading obedience. In order to please them, man must lay his very face in the dust. Of course, they have always been partial to the people who created them, and have generally shown their partiality by assisting those people to rob and destroy others, and to ravish their wives and daughters.

Nothing is so pleasing to these gods as the butchery of unbelievers. Nothing so enrages them, even now, as to have some one deny their existence.

Few nations have been so poor as to have but one god. Gods were made so easily, and the raw material cost so little, that generally the god market was fairly glutted, and heaven crammed with these phantoms. These gods not only attended to the skies, but were supposed to interfere in all the affairs of men. They presided over everybody and everything. They attended to every department. All was supposed to be under their immediate control. Nothing was too small—nothing too large; the falling of sparrows and the motions of the planets were alike attended to by these industrious and observing deities. From their starry thrones they frequently came to the earth for the purpose of imparting information to man. It is related of one that he came amid thunderings and lightnings in order to tell the people that they should not cook a kid in its mother's milk. Some left their shining abodes to tell women that they should, or should not, have children, to inform a priest how to cut and wear his apron, and to give directions as to the proper manner of cleaning the intestines of a bird.

When the people failed to worship one of these gods, or failed to feed and clothe his priests (which was much the same thing), he generally visited them with pestilence and famine. Sometimes he allowed some other nation to drag them into slavery—to sell their wives and children; but generally he glutted his vengeance by murdering their first-born. The priests always did their whole duty, not only in predicting these calamities, but in proving, when they did happen, that they were brought upon the people because they had not given quite enough to them.

These gods differed just as the nations differed; the greatest and most powerful had the most powerful gods, while the weaker ones were obliged to content themselves with the very off-scourings of the heavens. Each of these gods promised happiness here and hereafter to all his slaves, and threatened to eternally punish all who either disbelieved in his existence or suspected that some other god might be his superior; but to deny the existence of all gods was, and is, the crime of crimes. Redden your hands with human blood; blast by slander the fair fame of the innocent; strangle the smiling child upon its mother's knees; deceive, ruin, and desert the beautiful girl who loves and trusts you, and your case is not hopeless. For all this, and for all these you may be forgiven. For all this, and for all these, that bankrupt court established by the gospel will give you a discharge; but deny the existence of these divine ghosts, of these gods, and the sweet and tearful face of Mercy becomes livid with eternal hate. Heaven's golden gates are shut, and you, with an infinite curse ringing in your ears, with the brand of infamy upon your brow, commence your endless wanderings in the lurid gloom of hell—an immortal vagrant— an eternal outcast—a deathless convict.

One of these gods, and one who demands our love, our admiration, and our worship, and one who is worshiped, if mere heartless ceremony is worship, gave to his chosen people for their guidance, the following laws of war: "When thou comest nigh unto a city to fight against it, *then proclaim peace unto it. And it shall be if it make thee answer of peace, and open unto thee, then it shall be that all people that is found therein shall be tributaries unto thee, and they shall serve thee. And if it will make no peace with thee, but will make war against thee, then thou shalt besiege it. And when the Lord thy God hath delivered it into thy hands, thou shall smite every male thereof with the edge of the sword. But the women and the little ones, and the cattle, and all that is in the city, even all the spoil thereof, shalt thou take unto thyself, and thou shalt eat the spoil of thine enemies which the Lord thy God hath given thee. Thus shalt thou do unto all the cities which are very far off from thee, which are not of the cities of these nations. But of the cities of these people which the Lord thy God doth give thee for an inheritance, *thou shalt save alive nothing that breatheth.*"

Is it possible for man to conceive of anything more perfectly infamous? Can you believe that such directions were given by any being except an infinite fiend? Remember that the army receiving these instructions was one of invasion. Peace was offered upon condition that the people submitting should be the slaves of the invader; but if any should have the courage to defend their homes, to fight for the love of wife and child, then the sword was to spare none—not even the prattling, dimpled babe.

And we are called upon to worship such a God; to get upon our knees and tell him that he is good, that he is merciful, that he is just, that he is love. We are asked to stifle every noble sentiment of the soul, and to trample under foot all the sweet charities of the heart. Because we refuse to stultify ourselves—refuse to become liars—we are denounced, hated, traduced, and ostracized here, and this same god threatens to torment us in eternal fire the moment death allows him to fiercely clutch our naked helpless souls. Let the people hate, let the god threaten—we will educate them, and we will despise and defy him.

The book, called the Bible, is filled with passages equally horrible, unjust, and atrocious. This is the book to be read in schools in order to make our children loving, kind, and gentle! This is the book to be recognized in our Constitution as the source of all authority and justice!

Strange! that no one has ever been persecuted by the church for believing God bad, while hundreds of millions have been destroyed for thinking him good. The orthodox church never will forgive the Universalist for saying "God is love." It has always been considered as one of the very highest evidences of true and undefiled religion to insist that all men, women, and children deserve eternal damnation. It has always been heresy to say, "God will at last save all."

We are asked to justify these frightful passages, these infamous laws of war, because the Bible is the word of God. As a matter of fact, there never was, and there never can be, an argument even tending to prove the inspiration of any book whatever. In the absence of positive evidence, analogy, and experience, argument is simply impossible, and at the very best, can amount only to a useless agitation of the air. The instant we admit that a book is too sacred to be doubted, or even reasoned about, we are mental serfs. It is infinitely absurd to suppose that a god would address a communication to intelligent beings, and yet make it a crime, to be punished in eternal flames, for them to use their intelligence for the purpose of understanding his communication. If we have the right to use our reason, we certainly have the right to act in accordance with it, and no god can have the right to punish us for such action.

The doctrine that future happiness depends upon belief is monstrous. It is the infamy of infamies. The notion that faith in Christ is to be rewarded by an eternity of bliss, while a dependence upon reason, observation, and experience merits everlasting pain, is too absurd for refutation, and can be relieved only by that unhappy mixture of insanity and ignorance called "faith." What man, who ever thinks, can believe that blood can appease God? And yet, our entire system of religion is based upon that belief. The Jews pacified Jehovah with the blood of animals, and according to the Christian system, the blood of Jesus softened the heart of God a little, and rendered possible the salvation of a fortunate few. It is hard to conceive how the human mind can give assent to such terrible ideas, or how any sane man can read the Bible and still believe in the doctrine of inspiration.

Whether the Bible is true or false is of no consequence in comparison with the mental freedom of the race.

Salvation through slavery is worthless. Salvation from slavery is inestimable.

As long as man believes the Bible to be infallible, that book is his master. The civilization of this century is not the child of faith, but of unbelief—the result of free thought.

All that is necessary, as it seems to me, to convince any reasonable person that the Bible is simply and purely of human invention—of barbarian invention—is to read it. Read it as you would any other book; think of it as you would of any other; get the bandage of reverence from your eyes; drive from your heart the phantom of fear; push from the throne of your brain the cowled form of superstition—then read the Holy Bible, and you will be amazed that you ever, for one moment, supposed a being of infinite wisdom, goodness, and purity to be the author of such ignorance and of such atrocity.

Our ancestors not only had their god-factories, but they made devils as well. These devils were generally disgraced and fallen gods. Some had headed unsuccessful revolts; some had been caught sweetly reclining in the shadowy folds of some fleecy cloud, kissing the wife of the god of gods. These devils generally sympathized with man. There is in regard to them a most wonderful fact: In nearly all the theologies, mythologies, and religions, the devils have been much more humane and merciful than the gods. No devil ever gave one of his generals an order to kill children and to rip open the bodies of pregnant women. Such barbarities were always ordered by the good gods. The pestilences were sent by the most merciful gods. The frightful famine, during which the dying child with pallid lips sucked the withered bosom of a dead mother, was sent by the loving gods. No devil was ever charged with such fiendish brutality.

One of these gods, according to the account, drowned an entire world, with the exception of eight persons. The old, the young, the beautiful, and the helpless were remorsely devoured by the shoreless sea. This, the most fearful tragedy that the imagination of ignorant priests ever conceived, was the act, not of a devil, but of a god, so-called, whom men ignorantly worship unto this day. What a stain such an act would leave upon the character of a devil! One of the prophets of one of these gods, having in his power a captured king, hewed him in pieces in the sight of all the people. Was ever any imp of any devil guilty of such savagery?

One of these gods is reported to have given the following directions concerning human slavery: "If thou buy a Hebrew servant, six years shall he serve, and in the seventh he shall go out free for nothing. If he came in by himself, he shall go out by himself; if he were married, then his wife shall go out with him. If his master have given him a wife, and she have borne him sons or daughters, the wife and her children shall be her master's, and he shall go out by himself. And if the servant shall plainly say, I love my master, my wife, and my children; I will not go out free. Then his master shall bring him unto the judges; he shall also bring him unto the door, or unto the doorpost; and his master shall bore his ear through with an awl; and he shall serve him forever."

According to this, a man was given liberty upon condition

that he would desert forever his wife and children. Did any devil ever force upon a husband, upon a father, so cruel and so heartless an alternative? Who can worship such a god? Who can bend the knee to such a monster? Who can pray to such a fiend?

All these gods threatened to torment forever the souls of their enemies. Did any devil ever make so infamous a threat? The basest thing recorded of the devil is what he did concerning Job and his family, and that was done by the express permission of one of these gods, and to decide a little difference of opinion between their serene highnesses as to the character of "my servant Job."

The first account we have of the devil is found in that purely scientific book called Genesis, and is as follows: "Now the serpent was more subtile than any beast of the field which the Lord God had made, and he said unto the woman, Yea, hath God said, Ye shall not eat of the fruit of the trees of the garden? And the woman said unto the serpent, We may eat of the fruit of the trees of the garden; but of the fruit of the tree which is in the midst of the garden God hath said, Ye shall not eat of it, neither shall ye touch it, lest ye die. And the serpent said unto the woman, Ye shall not surely die. For God doth know that in the day ye eat thereof, then your eyes shall be opened and ye shall be as gods, knowing good and evil. And when the woman saw that the tree was good for food, and that it was pleasant to the eyes, and a tree to be desired to make one wise, she took of the fruit thereof and did eat, and gave also unto her husband with her, and he did eat. And the Lord God said, Behold the man is become as one of us, to know good and evil; and now, lest he put forth his hand, and take also of the tree of life and eat, and live forever. Therefore the Lord God sent him forth from the Garden of Eden to till the ground from which he was taken. So he drove out the man, and he placed at the east of the Garden of Eden cherubim and a flaming sword, which turned every way to keep the way of the tree of life."

According to this account the promise of the devil was fulfilled to the very letter. Adam and Eve did not die, and they did become as gods, knowing good and evil.

The account shows, however, that the gods dreaded education and knowledge then just as they do now. The church still faithfully guards the dangerous tree of knowledge, and has exerted in all ages her utmost power to keep mankind from eating the fruit thereof. The priests have never ceased repeating the old falsehood and the old threat: "Ye shall not eat of it, neither shall ye touch it, lest ye die." From every pulpit comes the same cry, born of the same fear: "Lest they eat and become as gods, knowing good and evil." For this reason, religion hates science, faith detests reason, theology is the sworn enemy of philosophy, and the church with its flaming sword still guards the hated tree, and like its supposed founder, curses to the lowest depths the brave thinkers who eat and become as gods.

If the account given in Genesis is really true, ought we not, after all, to thank this serpent? He was the first schoolmaster, the first advocate of learning, the first enemy of ignorance, the first to whisper in human ears the sacred word liberty, the creator of ambition, the author of modesty, of inquiry, of doubt, of investigation, of progress, and of civilization.

Give me the storm and tempest of thought and action, rather than the dead calm of ignorance and faith! Banish me from Eden when you will; but first let me eat of the fruit of the tree of knowledge!

Some nations have borrowed their gods; of this number, we are compelled to say, is our own. The Jews having ceased to exist as a nation, and having no further use for a god, our ancestors appropriated him and adopted their devil at the same time. This borrowed god is still an object of some adoration, and this adopted devil still excites the apprehensions of our people. He is still supposed to be setting his traps and snares for the purpose of catching our unwary souls, and is still, with reasonable success, waging the old war against our God.

To me, it seems easy to account for these ideas concerning gods and devils. They are a perfectly natural production. Man has created them all, and under the same circumstance would create them again. Man has not only created all these gods, but he has created them out of the materials by which he has been surrounded. Generally he has modeled them after himself, and has given them hands, heads, feet, eyes, ears, and organs of speech. Each nation made its gods and devils speak its language not only, but put in their mouths the same mistakes in history, geography, astronomy, and in all matters of fact, generally made by the people. No god was ever in advance of the nation that created him. The negroes represented their deities with black skins and curly hair. The Mongolian gave to his a yellow complexion and dark almond-shaped eyes. The Jews were not allowed to paint theirs, or we should have seen Jehovah with a full beard, an oval face, and an aquiline nose. Zeus was a perfect Greek, and Jove looked as though a member of the Roman senate. The gods of Egypt had the patient face and placid look of the loving people who made them. The gods of northern countries were represented warmly clad in robes of fur; those of the tropics were naked. The gods of India were often mounted upon elephants; those of some islanders were great swimmers, and the deities of the Arctic zone were passionately fond of whale's blubber. Nearly all people have carved or painted representations of their gods, and these representations were, by the lower classes, generally treated as the real gods, and to these images and idols they addressed prayers and offered sacrifice.

"In some countries, even at this day, if the people after long praying do not obtain their desires, they turn their images off as impotent gods, or upbraid them in a most reproachful manner, loading them with blows and curses. 'How now, dog of a spirit,' they say, 'we give you lodging in a magnificent temple, we gild you with gold, feed you with the choicest food, and offer incense to you; yet, after all this care, you are so ungrateful as to refuse us what we ask.' Hereupon they will pull the god down and drag him through the filth of the street. If, in the meantime, it happens that they obtain their request, then, with a great deal of ceremony, they wash him clean, carry him back and place him in his temple again, where they fall down and make excuses for what they have done. 'Of a truth,' they say, 'we were a little too hasty, and you were a little too long in your grant. Why should you bring this beating on yourself. But what is done cannot be undone. Let us not think of it any more. If you will forget what is past we will gild you over brighter again than before.' "

Man has never been at a loss for gods. He has worshiped almost everything, including the vilest and most disgusting beasts. He has worshiped fire, earth, air, water, light, stars, and for hundreds of ages prostrated himself before enormous snakes. Savage tribes often make gods of articles they get from civilized people. The Todas worship a cowbell. The Kotas worship two silver plates, which they regard as husband and wife, and another tribe manufactured a god out of a king of hearts.

Man, having always been the physical superior of woman, accounts for the fact that most of the high gods have been males. Had woman been the physical superior, the powers supposed to be the rulers of Nature would have been women, and instead of being represented in the apparel of man, they would have luxuriated in trains, low-necked dresses, laces, and back hair.

Nothing can be plainer than that each nation gives to its god its peculiar characteristics, and that every individual gives to his god his personal peculiarities.

Man has no ideas, and can have none, except those suggested by his surroundings. He cannot conceive of anything utterly unlike what he has seen or felt. He can exaggerate, diminish, combine, separate, deform, beautify, improve, multiply, and compare what he sees, what he feels, what he hears, and all of which he takes cognizance through the medium of the senses; but he cannot create. Having seen exhibitions of power, he can say omnipotent. Having lived, he can say immortality. Knowing something of time, he can say eternity. Conceiving something of intelligence, he can say God. Having seen exhibitions of malice, he can say devil. A few gleams of happiness having fallen athwart the gloom of his life, he can say heaven. Pain, in its numberless forms, having been experienced, he can say hell. Yet all these ideas have a foundation in fact, and only a foundation. The superstructure has been reared by exaggerating, diminishing, combining, separating, deforming, beautifying, improving, or multiplying realities, so that the edifice or fabric is but the incongruous grouping of what man has perceived through the medium of the senses. It is as though we should give to a lion the wings of an eagle, the hoofs of a bison, the tail of a horse, the pouch of a kangaroo, and the trunk of an elephant. We have in imagination created an impossible monster. And yet the various parts of this monster really exist. So it is with all the gods that man has made.

Beyond nature man cannot go even in thought—above nature he cannot rise—below nature he cannot fall.

Man, in his ignorance, supposed that all phenomena were produced by some intelligent powers, and with direct reference to him. To preserve friendly relations with these powers was, and still is, the object of all religions. Man knelt through fear and to implore assistance, or through gratitude for some favor which he supposed had been rendered. He endeavored by supplication to appease some being who, for some reason, had, as he believed, become enraged. The lightning and thunder terrified him. In the presence of the volcano he sank upon his knees. The great forests filled with wild and ferocious beasts, the monstrous serpents crawling in mysterious depths, the boundless sea, the flaming comets, the sinister eclipses, the awful calmness of the stars, and, more than all, the perpetual presence of death, convinced him that he was the sport and prey of unseen and malignant powers. The strange and frightful diseases to which he was subject, the freezings and burnings of fever, the contortions of epilepsy, the sudden palsies, the darkness of night, and the wild, terrible, and fantastic dreams that filled his brain, satisfied him that he was haunted and pursued by countless spirits of evil. For some reason he supposed that these spirits differed in power—that they were not all alike malevolent—that the higher controlled the lower, and that his very existence depended upon gaining the assistance of the more powerful. For this purpose he resorted to prayer, to flattery, to worship, and to sacrifice. These ideas appear to have been almost universal in savage man.

For ages all nations supposed that the sick and insane were possessed by evil spirits. For thousands of years the practice of medicine consisted in frightening these spirits away. Usually the priests would make the loudest and most discordant noises possible. They would blow horns, beat upon rude drums, clash cymbals, and in the meantime utter the most unearthly yells. If the noise remedy failed, they would impore the aid of some more powerful spirit.

To pacify these spirits was considered of infinite importance. The poor barbarian, knowing that men could be softened by gifts, gave to these spirits that which to him seemed of the most value. With bursting heart he would offer the blood of his dearest child. It was impossible for him to conceive of a god utterly unlike himself, and he naturally supposed that these powers of the air would be affected a little at the sight of so great and so deep a sorrow. It was with the barbarian then as with the civilized now—one class lived upon and made merchandise of the fears of another. Certain persons took it upon themselves to appease the gods, and to instruct the people in their duties to these unseen powers. This was the origin of the priesthood. The priest pretended to stand between the wrath of the gods and the helplessness of man. He was man's attorney at the court of heaven. He carried to the invisible world a flag of truce, a protest, and a request. He came back with a command, with authority, and with power. Man fell upon his knees before his own servant, and the priest, taking advantage of the awe inspired by his supposed influence with the gods, made of his fellow man a cringing hypocrite and slave. Even Christ, the supposed son of God, taught that persons were possessed of evil spirits, and frequently, according to the account, gave proof of his divine origin and mission by frightening droves of devils out of his unfortunate countrymen. Casting out devils was his principal employment, and the devils thus banished generally took occasion to acknowledge him as the true Messiah; which was not only very kind of them, but quite fortunate for him. The religious people have always regarded the testimony of these devils as perfectly conclusive, and the writers of the New Testament quote the words of these imps of darkness with great satisfaction.

The fact that Christ could withstand the temptations of the devil was considered as conclusive evidence that he was assisted by some god, or at least by some being superior to man. St. Matthew gives an account of an attempt made by the devil to tempt the supposed son of God; and it has always excited the wonder of Christians that the temptation was so nobly and heroically withstood. The account to which I refer is as follows:

"Then was Jesus led up of the spirit into the wilderness to be tempted of the devil. And when the tempter came to him, he said: 'If thou be the son of God, command that these stones be made bread.' But he answered, and said: 'It is written: man shall not live by bread alone, but by every word that proceedeth out of the mouth of God.' Then the devil taketh him up into the holy city and setteth him upon a pinnacle of the temple and saith unto him: 'If thou be the son of God, cast thyself down, for it is written, He shall give his angels charge concerning thee, lest at any time thou shalt dash thy foot against a stone.' Jesus said unto him: 'It is written again, thou shalt not tempt the Lord thy God.' Again the devil taketh him up into an exceeding high mountain and sheweth him all the kingdoms of the world and the glory of them, and saith unto him: 'All these will I give thee if thou wilt fall down and worship me.' "

The Christians now claim that Jesus was God. If he was God, of course the devil knew that fact, and yet, according to this account, the devil took the omnipotent God and placed him upon a pinnacle of the temple, and endeavored to induce him to dash himself against the earth. Failing in that, he took the creator, owner, and governor of the universe up into an exceeding high mountain, and offered him this world—this grain of sand—if he, the God of all the worlds, would fall down and worship him, a poor devil, without even a tax title to one foot of dirt! Is it possible the devil was such an idiot? Should any great credit be given to this deity for not being caught with such chaff? Think of it! The devil—the prince of sharpers—the king of cunning—the master of finesse, trying to bribe God with a grain of sand that belonged to God!

Is there in all the religious literature of the world anything more grossly absurd than this?

These devils, according to the Bible, were of various kinds— some could speak and hear, others were deaf and dumb. All could not be cast out in the same way. The deaf and dumb spirits were quite difficult to deal with. St. Mark tells of a gentleman who brought his son to Christ. The boy, it seems, was possessed of a dumb spirit, over which the disciples had no control. "Jesus said unto the spirit: 'Thou dumb and deaf spirit, I charge thee come out of him, and enter no more into him.' " Whereupon, the deaf spirit (having heard what was said) cried out (being dumb) and immediately vacated the premises. The ease with which Christ controlled this deaf and dumb spirit excited the wonder of his disciples, and they asked him privately why they could not cast that spirit out. To whom he replied: "This kind can come forth by nothing but prayer and fasting." Is there a Christian in the whole world who would believe such a story if found in any other book? The trouble is, these pious people shut up their reason, and then open their Bible.

In the olden times the existence of devils was universally ad-mitted. The people had no doubt upon that subject, and from such belief it followed as a matter of course, that a person, in order to vanquish these devils, had either to be a god, or to be assisted by one. All founders of religions have established their claims to divine origin by controlling evil spirits and suspend-ing the laws of nature. Casting out devils was a certificate of divin-ity. A prophet unable to cope with the powers of darkness was regarded with contempt. The utterance of the highest and noblest sentiments, the most blameless and holy life, commanded but little respect, unless accompanied by power to work miracles and command spirits.

This belief in good and evil powers had its origin in the fact that man was surrounded by what he was pleased to call good and evil phenomena. Phenomena affecting man pleasantly were ascribed to good spirits, while those affecting him unpleasantly or injuriously, were ascribed to evil spirits. It being admitted that all phenomena were produced by spirits, the spirits were divided according to the phenomena, and the phenomena were good or bad as they affected man. Good spirits were supposed to be the authors of good phenomena, and evil spirits of the evil—so that the idea of a devil has been as universal as the idea of a god.

Many writers maintain that an idea to become universal must be true; that all universal ideas are innate, and that innate ideas cannot be false. If the fact that an idea has been universal proves that it is innate, and if the fact that an idea is innate proves that it is correct, then the believers in innate ideas must admit that the evidence of a god superior to nature, and of a devil superior to nature, is exactly the same, and that the existence of such a devil must be as self-evident as the existence of such a god. The truth is, a god was inferred from good, and a devil from bad, phenomena. And it is just as natural and logical to suppose that a devil would cause happiness as to suppose that a god would produce misery. Consequently, if an intelligence, infinite and supreme, is the immediate author of all phenomena, it is difficult to determine whether such intelligence is the friend or enemy of man. If phenomena were all good, we might say they were all produced by a perfectly beneficent being. If they were all bad, we might say they were produced by a perfectly malevolent power; but, as phenomena are, as they affect man, both good and bad, they must be produced by different and antagonistic spirits; by one who is sometimes actuated by kindness, and sometimes by malice; or all must be produced of necessity, and without reference to their consequences upon man.

The foolish doctrine that all phenomena can be traced to the interference of good and evil spirits, has been, and still is, almost universal. That most people still believe in some spirit that can change the natural order of events, is proven by the fact that nearly all resort to prayer. Thousands, at this very moment, are probably imploring some supposed power to interfere in their behalf. Some want health restored; some ask that the loved and absent be watched over and protected, some pray for riches, some for rain, some want diseases stayed, some vainly ask for food, some ask for revivals, a few ask for more wisdom, and now and then one tells the Lord to do as he may think best. Thousands ask to be protected from the devil; some, like David, pray for revenge, and some implore even God, not to lead them into temptation. All these prayers rest upon, and are produced by, the idea that some power not only can, but probably will, change the order of the universe. This belief has been among the great majority of tribes and nations. All sacred books are filled with the accounts of such interferences, and our own Bible is no exception to this rule.

If we believe in a power superior to nature, it is perfectly natural to suppose that such power can and will interfere in the affairs of this world. If there is no interference, of what practical use can such power be? The Scriptures give us the most wonderful accounts of divine interference: Animals talk like men; springs gurgle from dry bones; the sun and moon stop in the heavens in order that General Joshua may have more time to murder; the shadow on a dial goes back ten degrees to convince a petty king of a barbarous people that he is not going to die of a boil; fire refuses to burn; water positively declines to seek its level, but stands up like a wall; grains of sand become lice; common walking sticks, to gratify a mere freak, twist themselves into serpents, and then swallow each other by way of exercise; murmuring streams, laughing at the attraction of gravitation, run up hill for years, following wandering tribes from a pure love of frolic; prophecy becomes altogether easier than history; the sons of God become enamored of the world's girls; women are changed into salt for the purpose of keeping a great event fresh in the minds of men; an excellent article of brimstone is imported from heaven free of duty; clothes refuse to wear out for forty years; birds keep restaurants and feed wandering prophets free of expense; bears tear children in pieces for laughing at old men without wigs; muscular development depends upon the length of one's hair; dead people come to life, simply to get a joke on their enemies and heirs; witches and wizards converse freely with the souls of the departed; and God himself becomes a stonecutter and engraver, after having been a tailor and dressmaker.

The veil between heaven and earth was always rent or lifted. The shadows of this world, the radiance of heaven, and the glare of hell mixed and mingled until man became uncertain as to which country he really inhabited. Man dwelt in an unreal world. He mistook his ideas, his dreams, for real things. His fears become terrible and malicious monsters. He lived in the midst of furies and fairies, nymphs and naiads, goblins and ghosts, witches and wizards, sprites and spooks, deities and devils. The obscure and gloomy depths were filled with claw and wing—with beak and hoof—with leering looks and sneering mouths—with the malice of deformity—with the cunning of hatred, and with all the slimy forms that fear can draw and paint upon the shadowy canvas of the dark.

It is enough to make one almost insane with pity to think what man in the long night has suffered; of the tortures he has endured, surrounded, as he supposed, by malignant powers and clutched by the fierce phantoms of the air. No wonder that he fell upon his trembling knees—that he built altars and reddened them even with his own blood. No wonder that he implored ignorant priests and impudent magicians for aid. No wonder that he crawled groveling in the dust to the temple's door, and there, in the insanity of despair, besought the deaf gods to hear his bitter cry of agony and fear.

The savage, as he emerges from a state of barbarism, gradually loses faith in his idols of wood and stone, and in their place puts a multitude of spirits. As he advances in knowledge, he generally discards the petty spirits, and in their stead believes in one, whom he supposes to be infinite and supreme. Supposing this great spirit to be superior to nature, he offers worship or flattery in exchange for assistance. At last, finding that he obtains no aid from this supposed deity—finding that every search after the absolute must of necessity end in failure—finding that man cannot by any possibility conceive of the conditionless—he begins to investigate the facts by which he is surrounded, and to depend upon himself.

The people are beginning to think, to reason, and to investigate. Slowly, painfully, but surely, the gods are being driven from the earth. Only upon rare occasions are they, even by the most religious, supposed to interfere in the affairs of men. In most matters we are at last supposed to be free. Since the invention of steamships and railways, so that the products of all countries can be easily interchanged, the gods have quit the business of producing famine. Now and then they kill a child because it is idolized by its parents. As a rule they have given up causing accidents on railroads, exploding boilers, and bursting kerosene lamps. Cholera, yellow fever, and smallpox are still considered heavenly weapons; but measles, itch, and ague are now attributed to natural causes. As a general thing, the gods have stopped drowning children, except as a punishment for violating the Sabbath. They still pay some attention to the affairs of kings, men of genius, and persons of great wealth; but ordinary people are left to shirk for themselves as best they may. In wars between great nations, the gods still interfere; but in prize fights, the best man with an honest referee is almost sure to win.

The church cannot abandon the idea of special providence. To give up that doctrine is to give up all. The church must insist that prayer is answered—that some power superior to nature hears and grants the request of the sincere and humble Christian, and that this same power in some mysterious way provides for all.

A devout clergyman sought every opportunity to impress upon the mind of his son the fact that God takes care of all his creatures; that the falling sparrow attracts his attention, and that his loving kindness is over all his works. Happening, one day, to see a crane wading in quest of food, the good man pointed out to his son the perfect adaptation of the crane to get his living in that manner.

"See," said he, "how his legs are formed for wading! What a long slender bill he has! Observe how nicely he folds his feet when putting them in or drawing them out of the water! He does not cause the slightest ripple. He is thus enabled to approach the fish without giving then any notice of his arrival." "My son," said he, "It is impossible to look at that bird without recognizing the design, as well as the goodness of God, in thus providing the means of subsistence." "Yes," replied the boy, "I think I see the goodness of God, at least so far as the crane is concerned; but after all, father, don't you think the arrangement is a little tough on the fish?"

Even the advanced religionist, although disbelieving in any great amount of interference by the gods in this age of the world, still thinks that in the beginning, some god made the laws governing the universe. He believes that in consequence of these laws a man can lift a greater weight with, than without, a lever; that this god so made matter, and so established the order of things, that two bodies cannot occupy the same space at the same time; so that a body once put in motion will keep moving until it is stopped; so that it is a greater distance around, than across a circle; so that a perfect square has four equal sides, instead of five or seven. He insists that it took a direct interposition of providence to make the whole greater than a part, and that had it not been for this power superior to nature, twice one might have been more than twice two, and sticks and strings might have had only one end apiece. Like the old Scotch divine, he thanks God that Sunday comes at the end instead of the middle of the week, and that death comes at the close instead of at the commencement of life, thereby giving us time to prepare for that holy day and that most solemn event. These religious people see nothing but design everywhere, and personal, intelligent interference in everything. They insist that the universe has been created, and that the adaptation of means to ends is perfectly apparent. They point us to the sunshine, to the flowers, to the April rain, and to all there is of beauty and of use in the world. Did it ever occur to them that a cancer is as beautiful in its development as is the reddest rose? That what they are pleased to call the adaptation of means to ends, is as apparent in the cancer as in the April rain? How beautiful the process of digestion! By what ingenious methods the blood is poisoned so that the cancer shall have food! By what wonderful contrivances the entire system of man is made to pay tribute to this divine and charming cancer! See by what admirable instrumentalities it feeds itself from the surrounding quivering, dainty flesh! See how it gradually but surely expands and grows! By what marvelous mechanism it is supplied with long and slender roots that reach out to the most secret nerves of pain for sustenance and life! What beautiful colors it presents! Seen through the microscope it is a miracle of order and beauty. All the ingenuity of man cannot stop its growth. Think of the amount of thought it must have required to invent a way by which the life of one man might be given to produce one cancer? Is it possible to look upon it and doubt that there is design in the universe, and that the inventor of this wonderful cancer must be infinitely powerful, ingenious, and good?

We are told that the universe was designed and created, and that it is absurd to suppose that matter has existed from eternity, but that it is perfectly self-evident that a god has.

If a god created the universe, then, there must have been a time when he commenced to create. Back of that time there must have been an eternity, during which there had existed nothing—absolutely nothing—except this supposed god. According to this theory, this god spent an eternity, so to speak, in an infinite vacuum, and in perfect idleness.

Admitting that a god did create the universe, the question then arises, of what did he create it? It certainly was not made of nothing. Nothing, considered in the light of a raw material, is a most decided failure. It follows, then, that the god must have made the universe out of himself, he being the only existence. The universe is material, and if it was made of god, the god must have been material. With this very thought in his mind, Anaximander of Miletus said: "Creation is the decomposition of the infinite."

It has been demonstrated that the earth would fall to the sun, only for the fact that it is attracted by other worlds, and those worlds must be attracted by other worlds still beyond them, and so on, without end. This proves the material universe to be infinite. If an infinite universe has been made out of an infinite god, how much of the god is left?

The idea of a creative deity is gradually being abandoned, and nearly all truly scientific minds admit that matter must have existed from eternity. It is indestructible, and the indestructible cannot be created. It is the crowning glory of our century to have demonstrated the indestructibility and the eternal persistence of force. Neither matter nor force can be increased nor diminished. Force cannot exist apart from matter. Matter exists only in connection with force, and consequently, a force apart from matter, and superior to nature, is a demonstrated impossibility.

Force, then, must have also existed from eternity, and could not have been created. Matter in its countless forms, from dead earth to the eyes of those we love, and force, in all its manifestations, from simple motion to the grandest thought, deny creation and defy control.

Thought is a form of force. We walk with the same force with which we think. Man is an organism, that changes several forms of force into thought-force. Man is a machine into which we put what we call food, and produce what we call thought. Think of that wonderful chemistry by which bread was changed into the divine tragedy of Hamlet!

A god must not only be material, but he must be an organism, capable of changing other forms of force into thought-force. This is what we call eating. Therefore, if the god thinks, he must eat, that is to say, he must of necessity have some means of supplying the force with which to think. It is impossible to conceive of a being who can eternally impart force to matter, and yet have no means of supplying the force thus imparted.

If neither matter nor force were created, what evidence have we, then, of the existence of a power superior to nature? The theologian will probably reply, "We have law and order, cause and effect, and beside all this, matter could not have put itself in motion."

Suppose, for the sake of the argument, that there is no being superior to nature, and that matter and force have existed from eternity. Now, suppose that two atoms should come together, would there be an effect? Yes. Suppose they came in exactly opposite directions with equal force, they would be stopped, to say the least. This would be an effect. If this is so, then you have matter, force, and effect without a being superior to nature. Now, suppose that two other atoms, just like the first two, should come together under precisely the same circumstances, would not the effect be exactly the same? Yes. Like causes, producing like effects, is what we mean by law and order. Then we have matter, force, effect, law, and order without a being superior to nature. Now, we know that every effect must also be a cause, and that every cause must be an effect. The atoms coming together did produce an effect, and as every effect must also be a cause, the effect produced by the collision of the atoms must as to something else have been a cause. Then we have matter, force, law, order, cause, and effect without a being superior to nature. Nothing is left for the supernatural but empty space. His throne is a void, and his boasted realm is without matter, without force, without law, without cause, and without effect.

But what put all this matter in motion? If matter and force have existed from eternity, then matter must have always been in motion. There can be no force without motion. Force is forever active, and there is, and there can be no cessation. If, therefore, matter and force have existed from eternity, so has motion. In the whole universe there is not even one atom in a state of rest.

A deity outside of nature exists in nothing, and is nothing. Nature embraces with infinite arms all matter and all force. That which is beyond her grasp is destitute of both, and can hardly be worth the worship and adoration even of a man.

There is but one way to demonstrate the existence of a power independent of and superior to nature, and that is by breaking, if only for one moment, the continuity of cause and effect. Pluck from the endless chain of existence one little link; stop for one instant the grand procession, and you have shown beyond all contradiction that nature has a master. Change the fact, just for one second, that matter attracts matter, and a god appears.

The rudest savage has always known this fact, and for that reason always demanded the evidence of miracle. The founder of a religion must be able to turn water into wine—cure with a word the blind and lame, and raise with a simple touch the dead to life. It was necessary for him to demonstrate to the satisfaction of his barbarian disciple, that he was superior to nature. In times of ignorance this was easy to do. The credulity of the savage was almost boundless. To him the marvelous was the beautiful, the mysterious was sublime. Consequently, every religion has for its foundation a miracle—that is to say, a violation of nature—that is to say, a falsehood.

No one, in the world's whole history, ever attempted to substantiate a truth by a miracle. Truth scorns the assistance of miracle. Nothing but falsehood ever attested itself by signs and wonders. No miracle ever was performed, and no sane man ever thought he performed one, and until one is performed, there can be no evidence of the existence of any power superior to, and independent of nature.

The church wishes us to believe. Let the church, or one of its intellectual saints, perform a miracle, and we will believe. We are told that nature has a superior. Let this superior, for one single instant, control nature, and we will admit the truth of your assertions.

We have heard talk enough. We have listened to all the drowsy, idealess, vapid sermons that we wish to hear. We have read your Bible and the works of your best minds. We have heard your prayers, your solemn groans, and your reverential amens. All these amount to less than nothing. We want one fact. We beg at the doors of your churches for just one little fact. We pass our hats along your pews and under your pulpits and implore you for just one fact. We know all about your moldy wonders and your stale miracles. We want a this year's fact. We ask only one. Give us one fact for charity. Your miracles are too ancient. The witnesses have been dead for nearly two thousand years. Their reputation for "truth and veracity" in the neighborhood where they resided is wholly unknown to us. Give us a new miracle, and substantiate it by witnesses who still have the cheerful habit of living in this world. Do not send us to Jericho to hear the winding horns, nor put us in the fire with Shadrach, Meshech, and Abednego. Do not compel us to navigate the sea with Captain Jonah, nor dine with Mr. Ezekiel. There is no sort of use in sending us fox-hunting with Samson. We have positively lost all interest in that little speech so eloquently delivered by Balaam's inspired donkey. It is worse than useless to show us fishes with money in their mouths, and call our attention to vast multitudes stuffing themselves with five crackers and two sardines. We demand a new miracle, and we demand it now. Let the church furnish at least one, or forever hold her peace.

In the olden time, the church, by violating the order of nature, proved the existence of her God. At that time miracles were performed with the most astonishing ease. They became so common that the church ordered her priests to desist. And now this same church—the people having found some little sense—admits, not only, that she cannot perform a miracle, but insists that the absence of miracle—the steady, unbroken march of cause and effect, proves the existence of a power superior to nature. The fact is, however, that the indissoluble chain of cause and effect proves exactly the contrary.

Sir William Hamilton, one of the pillars of modern theology, in discussing this very subject, uses the following language: "The phenomena of matter taken by themselves, so far from warranting any inference to the existence of a god, would on the contrary ground even an argument to his negation. The phenomena of the material world are subjected to immutable laws, are produced and reproduced in the same invariable succession, and manifest only the blind force of a mechanical necessity."

Nature is but an endless series of efficient causes. She cannot create, but she eternally transforms. There was no beginning, and there can be no end.

The best minds, even in the religious world, admit that in material nature there is no evidence of what they are pleased to call a god. They find their evidence in the phenomena of intelligence, and very innocently assert that intelligence is above, and in fact, opposed to nature. They insist that man, at least, is a special creation; that he has somewhere in his brain a divine spark, a little portion of the "Great First Cause." They say that matter cannot produce thought; but that thought can produce matter. They tell us that man has intelligence, and therefore there must be an intelligence greater than his. Why not say, God has intelligence, therefore there must be an intelligence greater than his? So far as we know, there is no intelligence apart from matter. We cannot conceive of thought, except as produced within a brain.

The science, by means of which they demonstrate the existence of an impossible intelligence, and an incomprehensible power, is called metaphysics or theology. The theologians admit that the phenomena of matter tend, at least, to disprove the existence of any power superior to nature, because in such phenomena we see nothing but an endless chain of efficient causes—nothing but the force of a mechanical necessity. They therefore appeal to what they denominate the phenomena of mind to establish this superior power.

The trouble is, that in the phenomena of mind we find the same endless chain of efficient causes; the same mechanical necessity. Every thought must have had an efficient cause. Every motive, every desire, every fear, hope, and dream must have been necessarily produced. There is no room in the mind of man for providence or chance. The facts and forces governing thought are as absolute as those governing the motions of the planets. A poem is produced by the forces of nature, and is as necessarily and naturally produced as mountains and seas. You will seek in vain for a thought in man's brain without its efficient cause. Every mental operation is the necessary result of certain facts and conditions. Mental phenomena are considered more complicated than those of matter, and consequently more mysterious. Being more mysterious, they are considered better evidence of the existence of a god. No one infers a god from the simple, from the known, from what is understood, but from the complex, from the unknown, and incomprehensible. Our ignorance is God; what we know is science.

When we abandon the doctrine that some infinite being created matter and force, and enacted a code of laws for their government, the idea of interference will be lost. The real priest will then be, not the mouthpiece of some pretended deity, but the interpreter of nature. From that moment the church ceases to exist. The tapers will die out upon the dusty altar; the moths will eat the fading velvet of pulpit and pew; the Bible will take its place with the Shastras, Puranas, Vedas, Eddas, Sagas, and Korans; and the fetters of a degrading faith will fall from the minds of men.

"But," says the religionist, "you cannot explain everything; you cannot understand everything; and that which you cannot explain, that which you do not comprehend, is my God"

We are explaining more every day. We are understanding more every day; consequently your God is growing smaller every day.

Nothing daunted, the religionist then insists that nothing can exist without a cause, except cause, and that this uncaused cause is God.

To this we again reply: Every cause must produce an effect, because until it does produce an effect, it is not a cause. Every effect must in its turn become a cause. Therefore, in the nature of things, there cannot be a last cause, for the reason that a so-called last cause would necessarily produce an effect, and that effect must of necessity become a cause. The converse of these propositions must be true. Every effect must have had a cause, and every cause must have been an effect. Therefore there could have been no first cause. A first cause is just as impossible as a last effect.

Beyond the universe there is nothing, and within the universe the supernatural does not and cannot exist.

The moment these great truths are understood and admitted, a belief in general or special providence become impossible. From that instant men will cease their vain efforts to please an imaginary being, and will give their time and attention to the affairs of this world. They will abandon the idea of attaining any object by prayer and supplication. The element of uncertainty will, in a great measure, be removed from the domain of the future, and man, gathering courage from a succession of victories over the obstructions of nature, will attain a serene grandeur unknown to the disciples of any superstition. The plans of mankind will no longer be interfered with by the finger of a supposed omnipotence, and no one will believe that nations or individuals are protected or destroyed by any deity whatever. Science, freed from the chains of pious custom and evangelical prejudice, will, within her sphere, be supreme. The mind will investigate without reverence, and publish its conclusions without fear. Agassiz will no longer hesitate to declare the Mosaic cosmogony utterly inconsistent with the demonstrated truths of geology, and will cease pretending any reverence for the Jewish Scriptures. The moment science succeeds in rendering the church powerless for evil, the real thinkers will be outspoken. The little flags of truce carried by timid philosophers will disappear, and the cowardly parley will give place to victory— lasting and universal.

If we admit that some infinite being has controlled the destinies of persons and peoples, history becomes a most cruel and bloody farce. Age after age, the strong have trampled upon the weak; the crafty and heartless have ensnared and enslaved the simple and innocent; and nowhere, in all the annals of mankind, has any god succored the oppressed.

Man should cease to expect aid from on high. By this time he should know that heaven has no ear to hear, and no hand to help. The present is the necessary child of the past. There has been no chance, and there can be no interference.

If abuses are destroyed, man must destroy them. If slaves are freed, man must free them. If new truths are discovered, man must discover them. If the naked are clothed; if the hungry are fed; if justice is done; if labor is rewarded; if superstition is driven from the mind; if the defenseless are protected; and if the right finally triumphs, all must be the work of man. The grand victories of the future must be won by man, and by man alone.

Nature, so far as we can discern, without passion and without intention, forms, transforms, and retransforms forever. She neither weeps nor rejoices. She produces man without purpose, and obliterates him without regret. She knows no distinction between the beneficial and the hurtful. Poison and nutrition, pain and joy, life and death, smiles and tears are alike to her. She is neither merciful nor cruel. She cannot be flattered by worship nor melted by tears. She does not know even the attitude of prayer. She appreciates no difference between poison in the fangs of snakes and mercy in the hearts of men. Only through man does nature take cognizance of the good, the true, and the beautiful; and, so far as we know, man is the highest intelligence.

And yet man continues to believe that there is some power independent of and superior to nature, and still endeavors, by form, ceremony, supplication, hypocrisy, and sacrifice, to obtain its aid. His best energies have been wasted in the service of this phantom. The horrors of witchcraft were all born of an ignorant belief in the existence of a totally depraved being superior to nature, acting in perfect independence of her laws; and all religious superstition has had for its basis a belief in at least two beings, one good and the other bad, both of whom could arbitrarily change the order of the universe. The history of religion is simply the story of man's efforts in all ages to avoid one of these powers, and to pacify the other. Both powers have inspired little else than abject fear. The cold, calculating sneer of the devil, and the frown of God were equally terrible. In any event, man's fate was to be arbitrarily fixed forever by an unknown power superior to all law, and to all fact. Until this belief is thrown aside, man must consider himself the slave of phantom masters—neither of whom promise liberty in this world nor in the next.

Man must learn to rely upon himself. Reading Bibles will not protect him from the blasts of winter, but houses, fires, and clothing will. To prevent famine, one plow is worth a million sermons, and even patent medicines will cure more diseases than all the prayers uttered since the beginning of the world.

Although many eminent men have endeavored to harmonize necessity and free will, the existence of evil, and the infinite power and goodness of God, they have succeeded only in producing learned and ingenious failures. Immense efforts have been made to reconcile ideas utterly inconsistent with the facts by which we are surrounded, and all persons who have failed to perceive the pretended reconciliation have been denounced as infidels, atheists, and scoffers. The whole power of the church has been brought to bear against philosophers and scientists in order to compel a denial of the authority of demonstration, and to induce some Judas to betray Reason, one of the saviors of mankind.

During that frightful period known as the "Dark Ages," Faith reigned, with scarcely a rebellious subject. Her temples were "carpeted with knees," and the wealth of nations adorned her countless shrines. The great painters prostituted their genius to immortalize her vagaries, while the poets enshrined them in song. At her bidding, man covered the earth with blood. The scales of Justice were turned with her gold, and for her use were invented all the cunning instruments of pain. She built cathedrals for God, and dungeons for men. She peopled the clouds with angels and the earth with slaves. For centuries the world was retracing its steps— going steadily back toward barbaric night! A few infidels—a few heretics cried "Halt!" to the great rabble of ignorant devotion, and made it possible for the genius of the nineteenth century to revolutionize the cruel creeds and superstitions of mankind.

The thoughts of man, in order to be of any real worth, must be free. Under the influence of fear the brain is paralyzed, and instead of bravely solving a problem for itself, tremblingly adopts the solution of another. As long as a majority of men will cringe to the very earth before some petty prince or king, what must be the infinite abjectness of their little souls in the presence of their supposed creator and God? Under such circumstances, what can their thoughts be worth?

The originality of repetition, and the mental vigor of acquiescence, are all that we have any right to expect from the Christian world. As long as every question is answered by the word "God," scientific inquiry is simply impossible. As fast as phenomena are satisfactorily explained, the domain of the power supposed to be superior to nature must decrease, while the horizon of the known must as constantly continue to enlarge.

It is no longer satisfactory to account for the fall and rise of nations by saying, "It is the will of God." Such an explanation puts ignorance and education upon an exact equality, and does away with the idea of really accounting for anything whatever.

Will the religionist pretend that the real end of science is to ascertain how and why God acts? Science, from such a standpoint, would consist in investigating the law of arbitrary action, and in a grand endeavor to ascertain the rules necessarily obeyed by infinite caprice.

From a philosophical point of view, science is knowledge of the laws of life; of the conditions of happiness; of the facts by which we are surrounded; and the relations we sustain to men and things—by means of which, man, so to speak, subjugates nature and bends the elemental powers to his will, making blind force the servant of his brain.

A belief in special providence does away with the spirit of investigation, and is inconsistent with personal effort. Why should man endeavor to thwart the designs of God? Which of you, by taking thought, can add one cubit to his stature? Under the influence of this belief, man, basking in the sunshine of a delusion, considers the lilies of the field and refuses to take any thought for the morrow. Believing himself in the power of an infinite being, who can, at any moment, dash him to the lowest hell or raise him to the highest heaven, he necessarily abandons the idea of accomplishing anything by his own efforts. As long as this belief was general, the world was filled with ignorance, superstition, and misery. The energies of man were wasted in a vain effort to obtain the aid of this power, supposed to be superior to nature. For countless ages, even men were sacrificed upon the altar of this impossible god. To please him, mothers have shed the blood of their own babes; martyrs have chanted triumphant songs in the midst of flame; priests have gorged themselves with blood; nuns have forsworn the ecstasies of love; old men have tremblingly implored; women have sobbed and entreated; every pain has been endured; and every horror has been perpetrated.

Through the dim long years that have fled, humanity has suffered more than can be conceived. Most of the misery has been endured by the weak, the loving, and the innocent. Woman have been treated like poisonous beasts, and little children trampled upon as though they had been vermin. Numberless altars have been reddened, even with the blood of babes; beautiful girls have been given to slimy serpents; whole races of men doomed to centuries of slavery; and everywhere there has been outrage beyond the power of genius to express. During all these years the suffering have supplicated; the withered lips of famine have prayed; the pale victims have implored; and Heaven has been deaf and blind.

Of what use have the gods been to man?

It is no answer to say that some god created the world, established certain laws, and then turned his attention to other matters, leaving his children weak, ignorant, and unaided, to fight the battle of life alone. It is no solution to declare that in some other world this god will render a few, or even all, his subjects happy. What right have we to expect that a perfectly wise, good, and powerful being will ever do better than he has done, and is doing? The world is filled with imperfections. If it was made by an infinite being, what reason have we for saying that he will render it nearer perfect than it now is? If the infinite "Father" allows a majority of his children to live in ignorance and wretchedness now, what evidence is there that he will ever improve their condition? Will God have more power? Will he become more merciful? Will his love for his poor creatures increase? Can the conduct of infinite wisdom, power, and love ever change? Is the infinite capable of any improvement whatever?

We are informed by the clergy that this world is a kind of school; that the evils by which we are surrounded are for the purpose of developing our souls, and that only by suffering can men become pure, strong, virtuous, and grand.

Supposing this to be true, what is to become of those who die in infancy? The little children, according to this philosophy, can never be developed. They were so unfortunate as to escape the ennobling influences of pain and misery, and as a consequence, are doomed to an eternity of mental inferiority. If the clergy are right on this question, none are so unfortunate as the happy, and we should envy only the suffering and distressed. If evil is necessary to the development of man, in this life, how is it possible for the soul to improve in the perfect joy of Paradise?

Since Paley found his watch, the argument of "design" has been relied upon as unanswerable. The church teaches that this world, and all that it contains, were created substantially as we now see them; that the grasses, the flowers, the trees, and all animals, including man, were special creations, and that they sustain no necessary relation to each other. The most orthodox will admit that some earth has been washed into the sea; that the sea has encroached a little upon the land, and that some mountains may be a trifle lower than in the morning of creation. The theory of gradual development was unknown to our fathers; the idea of evolution did not occur to them. Our fathers looked upon the then arrangement of things as the primal arrangement. The earth appeared to them fresh from the hands of a deity. They knew nothing of the slow evolutions of countless years, but supposed that the almost infinite variety of vegetable and animal forms had existed from the first.

Suppose that upon some island we should find a man a million years of age, and suppose that we should find him in the possession of a most beautiful carriage, constructed upon the most perfect model. And suppose, further, that he should tell us that it was the result of several hundred thousand years of labor and of thought; that for fifty thousand years he used as flat a log as he could find, before it occurred to him, that by splitting the log, he could have the same surface with only half the weight; that it took him many thousand years to invent wheels for this log; that the wheels he first used were solid, and that fifty thousand years of thought suggested the use of spokes and tire; that for many centuries he used the wheels without linchpins; that it took a hundred thousand years more to think of using four wheels, instead of two; that for ages he walked behind the carriage, when going downhill, in order to hold it back, and that only by a lucky chance he invented the tongue; would we conclude that this man, from the very first, had been an infinitely ingenious and perfect mechanic? Suppose we found him living in an elegant mansion, and he should inform us that he lived in that house for five hundred thousand years before he thought of putting on a roof, and that he had but recently invented windows and doors; would we say that from the beginning he had been an infinitely accomplished and scientific architect?

Does not an improvement in the things created show a corresponding improvement in the creator?

Would an infinitely wise, good, and powerful God, intending to produce man, commence with the lowest possible forms of life; with the simplest organism that can be imagined, and during immeasurable periods of time, slowly and almost imperceptibly improve upon the rude beginning, until man was evolved? Would countless ages thus be wasted in the production of awkward forms, afterwards abandoned? Can the intelligence of man discover the least wisdom in covering the earth with crawling, creeping horrors, that live only upon the agonies and pangs of others? Can we see the propriety of so constructing the earth, that only an insignificant portion of its surface is capable of producing an intelligent man? Who can appreciate the mercy of so making the world that all animals devour animals; so that every mouth is a slaughterhouse, and every stomach a tomb? Is it possible to discover infinite intelligence and love in universal and eternal carnage?

What would we think of a father, who should give a farm to his children, and before giving them possession should plant upon it thousands of deadly shrubs and vines; should stock it with ferocious beasts, and poisonous reptiles; should take pains to put a few swamps in the neighborhood to breed malaria; should so arrange matters, that the ground would occasionally open and swallow a few of his darlings; and besides all this, should establish a few volcanoes in the immediate vicinity, that might at any moment overwhelm his children with rivers of fire? Suppose that this father neglected to tell his children which of the plants were deadly; that the reptiles were poisonous; failed to say anything about the earthquakes, and kept the volcano business a profound secret; would we pronounce him angel or fiend?

And yet this is exactly what the orthodox God has done.

According to the theologians, God prepared this globe expressly for the habitation of his loved children, and yet he filled the forests with ferocious beasts, placed serpents in every path, stuffed the world with earthquakes, and adorned its surface with mountains of flame.

Notwithstanding all this, we are told that the world is perfect; that it was created by a perfect being, and is therefore necessarily perfect. The next moment, these same persons will tell us that the world was cursed; covered with brambles, thistles and thorns; and that man was doomed to disease and death, simply because our poor, dear mother ate an apple contrary to the command of an arbitrary God.

A very pious friend of mine, having heard that I had said the world was full of imperfections, asked me if the report was true. Upon being informed that it was, he expressed great surprise that any one could be guilty of such presumption. He said that, in his judgment, it was impossible to point out an imperfection. "Be kind enough," said he, "to name even one improvement that you could make, if you had the power." "Well," said I, "I would make good health catching, instead of disease." The truth is, it is impossible to harmonize all the ills, and pains, and agonies of this world with the idea that we were created by, and are watched over and protected by an infinitely wise, powerful, and beneficent God, who is superior to and independent of nature.

The clergy, however, balance all the real ills of this life with the expected joys of the next. We are assured that all is perfection in heaven—there the skies are cloudless—there all is serenity and peace. Here empires may be overthrown; dynasties may be extinguished in blood; millions of slaves may toil 'neath the fierce rays of the sun, and the cruel strokes of the lash; yet all is happiness in heaven. Pestilences may strew the earth with corpses of the loved; the survivors may bend above them in agony—yet the placid bosom of heaven is unruffled. Children may expire vainly asking for bread; babes may be devoured by serpents, while the gods sit smiling in the clouds. The innocent may languish unto death in the obscurity of dungeons; brave men and heroic women may be changed to ashes at the bigot's stake, while heaven is filled with song and joy. Out on the wide sea, in darkness and storm, the shipwrecked struggle with the cruel waves while the angels play upon their golden harps. The streets of the world are filled with the diseased, the deformed, and the helpless; the chambers of pain are crowded with the pale forms of the suffering, while the angels float and fly in the happy realms of day. In heaven they are too happy to have sympathy; too busy singing to aid the imploring and distressed. Their eyes are blinded; their ears are stopped and their hearts are turned to stone by the infinite selfishness of joy. The saved mariner is too happy when he touches the shore to give a moment's thought to his drowning brothers. With the indifference of happiness, with the contempt of bliss, heaven barely glances at the miseries of earth. Cities are devoured by the rushing lava; the earth opens and thousands perish; women raise their clasped hands towards heaven, but the gods are too happy to aid their children. The smiles of the deities are unacquainted with the tears of men. The shouts of heaven drown the sobs of earth.

Having shown how man created gods, and how he became the trembling slave of his own creation, the questions naturally arise: How did he free himself even a little, from these monarchs of the sky, from these despots of the clouds, from this aristocracy of the air? How did he, even to the extent that he has, outgrow his ignorant, abject terror, and throw off the yoke of superstition?

Probably, the first thing that tended to disabuse his mind was the discovery of order, of regularity, of periodicity in the universe. From this he began to suspect that everything did not happen purely with reference to him. He noticed that whatever he might do, the motions of the planets were always the same; that eclipses were periodical; and that even comets came at certain intervals. This convinced him that eclipses and comets had nothing to do with him, and that his conduct had nothing to do with them. He perceived that they were not caused for his benefit or injury. He thus learned to regard them with admiration instead of fear. He began to suspect that famine was not sent by some enraged and revengeful deity, but resulted often from the neglect and ignorance of man. He learned that diseases were not produced by evil spirits. He found that sickness was occasioned by natural causes, and could be cured by natural means. He demonstrated, to his own satisfaction at least, that prayer is not a medicine. He found by sad experience that his gods were of no practical use, as they never assisted him, except when he was perfectly able to help himself. At last, he began to discover that his individual action had nothing whatever to do with strange appearances in the heavens; that it was impossible for him to be bad enough to cause a whirlwind, or good enough to stop one. After many centuries of thought, he about half concluded that making mouths at a priest would not necessarily cause an earthquake. He noticed, and no doubt with considerable astonishment, that very good men were occasionally struck by lightning, while very bad ones escaped. He was frequently forced to the painful conclusion (and it is the most painful to which any human being ever was forced) that the right did not always prevail. He noticed that the gods did not interfere in behalf of the weak and innocent. He was now and then astonished by seeing an unbeliever in the enjoyment of most excellent health. He finally ascertained that there could be no possible connection between an unusually severe winter and his failure to give a sheep to a priest. He began to suspect that the order of the universe was not constantly being changed to assist him because he repeated a creed. He observed that some children would steal after having been regularly baptized. He noticed a vast difference between religion and justice, and that the worshipers of the same god took delight in cutting each other's throats. He saw that these religious disputes filled the world with hatred and slavery. At last he had the courage to suspect that no god at any time interferes with the order of events. He learned a few facts, and these facts positively refused to harmonize with the ignorant superstitions of his fathers. Finding his sacred books incorrect and false in some particulars, his faith in their authenticity began to be shaken; finding his priests ignorant upon some points, he began to lose respect for the cloth. This was the commencement of intellectual freedom.

The civilization of man has increased just to the same extent that religious power has decreased. The intellectual advancement of man depends upon how often he can exchange an old superstition for a new truth. The church never enabled a human being to make even one of these exchanges; on the contrary, all her power has been used to prevent them. In spite, however, of the church, man found that some of his religious conceptions were wrong. By reading his Bible, he found that the ideas of his God were more cruel and brutal than those of the most depraved savage. He also discovered that this holy book was filled with ignorance, and that it must have been written by persons wholly unacquainted with the nature of the phenomena by which we are surrounded; and now and then, some man had the goodness and courage to speak his honest thoughts. In every age some thinker, some doubter, some investigator, some hater of hypocrisy, some despiser of sham, some brave lover of the right, has gladly, proudly, and heroically braved the ignorant fury of superstition for the sake of man and truth. These divine men were generally torn in pieces by the worshipers of the gods. Socrates was poisoned because he lacked reverence for some of the deities. Christ was crucified by a religious rabble for the crime of blasphemy. Nothing is more gratifying to a religionist than to destroy his enemies at the command of God. Religious persecution springs from a due admixture of love towards God and hatred towards man.

The terrible religious wars that inundated the world with blood tended at least to bring all religion into disgrace and hatred. Thoughtful people began to question the divine origin of a religion that made its believers hold the rights of others in absolute contempt. A few began to compare Christianity with the religions of heathen people, and were forced to admit that the difference was hardly worth dying for. They also found that other nations were even happier and more prosperous than their own. They began to suspect that their religion, after all, was not of much real value.

For three hundred years the Christian world endeavored to rescue from the "Infidel" the empty sepulcher of Christ. For three hundred years the armies of the cross were baffled and beaten by the victorious hosts of an impudent imposter. This immense fact sowed the seeds of distrust throughout all Christendom, and millions began to lose confidence in a God who had been vanquished by Mohammed. The people also found that commerce made friends where religion made enemies, and that religious zeal was utterly incompatible with peace between nations or individuals. They discovered that those who loved the gods most were apt to love men least; that the arrogance of universal forgiveness was amazing; that the most malicious had the effrontery to pray for their enemies; and that humility and tyranny were the fruit of the same tree.

For ages, a deadly conflict has been waged between a few brave men and women of thought and genius upon the one side, and the great ignorant religious mass on the other. This is the war between Science and Faith. The few have appealed to reason, to honor, to law, to freedom, to the known, and to happiness here in this world. The many have appealed to prejudice, to fear, to miracle, to slavery, to the unknown, and to misery hereafter. The few have said "Think!" The many have said "Believe!"

The first doubt was the womb and cradle of progress, and from the first doubt, man has continued to advance. Men began to investigate, and the church began to oppose. The astronomer scanned the heavens, while the church branded his grand forehead with the word "Infidel"; and now, not a glittering star in all the vast expanse bears a Christian name. In spite of all religion, the geologist penetrated the earth, read her history in books of stone, and found, hidden within her bosom, souvenirs of all the ages. Old ideas perished in the retort of the chemist, and useful truths took their places. One by one religious conceptions have been placed in the crucible of science, and thus far, nothing but dross has been found. A new world has been discovered by the microscope; everywhere has been found the infinite; in every direction man has investigated and explored and nowhere, in earth or stars, has been found the footstep of any being superior to or independent of nature. Nowhere has been discovered the slightest evidence of any interference from without.

These are the sublime truths that enabled man to throw off the yoke of superstition. These are the splendid facts that snatched the scepter of authority from the hands of priests.

In that vast cemetery, called the past, are most of the religions of men, and there, too, are nearly all their gods. The sacred temples of India were ruins long ago. Over column and cornice; over the painted and pictured walls, cling and creep the trailing vines. Brahma, the golden, with four heads and four arms; Vishnu, the somber, the punisher of the wicked, with his three eyes, his crescent, and his necklace of skulls; Siva, the destroyer, red with seas of blood; Kali, the goddess; Draupadi, the white-armed; and Chrishna, the Christ, all passed away and left the throne of heaven desolate. Along the banks of the sacred Nile, Isis no longer wandering weeps, searching for the dead Osiris. The shadow of Typhon's scowl falls no more upon the waves. The sun rises as of yore, and his golden beams still smite the lips of Memnon, but Memnon is as voiceless as the Sphinx. The sacred fanes are lost in desert sands; the dusty mummies are still waiting for the resurrection promised by their priests; and the old beliefs, wrought in curiously sculptured stone, sleep in the mystery of a language lost and dead. Odin, the author of life and soul, Vili and Ve, and the mighty giant Ymir, strode long ago from the icy halls of the North; and Thor, with iron glove and glittering hammer, dashes mountains to the earth no more. Broken are the circles and cromlechs of the ancient Druids; fallen upon the summits of the hills, and covered with the centuries' moss, are the sacred cairns. The divine fires of Persia and of the Aztecs have died out in the ashes of the past, and there is none to rekindle, and none to feed the holy flames. The harp of Orpheus is still; the drained cup of Bacchus has been thrown aside; Venus lies dead in stone, and her white bosom heaves no more with love. The streams still murmur, but no naiads bathe; the trees still wave, but in the forest aisles no dryads dance. The gods have flown from high Olympus. Not even the beautiful women can lure them back, and Danae lies unnoticed, naked to the stars. Hushed forever are the thunders of Sinai; lost are the voices of the prophets, and the land once flowing with milk and honey, is but a desert waste. One by one, the myths have faded from the clouds: one by one, the phantom host has disappeared, and one by one, facts, truths, and realities have taken their places. The supernatural has almost gone, but the natural remains. The gods have fled, but man is here.

Nations, like individuals, have their periods of youth, of manhood, and decay. Religions are the same. The same inexorable destiny awaits them all. The gods created by the nations must perish with their creators. They were created by men, and like men, they must pass away. The deities of one age are the by-words of the next. The religion of our day, and country, is no more exempt from the sneer of the future than the others have been. When India was supreme, Brahma sat upon the world's throne. When the scepter passed to Egypt, Isis and Osiris received the homage of mankind. Greece, with her fierce valor, swept to empire, and Zeus put on the purple of authority. The earth trembled with the tread of Rome's intrepid sons, and Jove grasped with mailed hand the thunderbolts of heaven. Rome fell, and Christians from her territory, with the red sword of war, carved out the ruling nations of the world, and now Christ sits upon the old throne. Who will be his successor?

Day by day, religious conceptions grow less and less intense. Day by day, the old spirit dies out of book and creed. The burning enthusiasm, the quenchless zeal of the early church have gone, never, never to return. The ceremonies remain, but the ancient faith is fading out of the human heart. The worn-out arguments fail to convince, and denunciations that once blanched the faces of a race excite in us only derision and disgust. As time rolls on, the miracles grow mean and small, and the evidences our fathers thought conclusive utterly fail to satisfy us. There is an "irrepressible conflict" between religion and science, and they cannot peaceably occupy the same brain nor the same world.

While utterly discarding all creeds, and denying the truth of all religions, there is neither hope in my heart nor upon my lips a sneer for the hopeful, loving, and tender souls who believe that from all this discord will result a perfect harmony; that every evil will in some mysterious way become a good; and that above and over all there is a being who, in some way, will reclaim and glorify every one of the children of men; but for those who heartlessly try to prove that salvation is almost impossible; that damnation is almost certain; that the highway of the universe leads to hell; who fill life with fear and death with horror; who curse the cradle and mock the tomb, it is impossible to entertain other than feelings of pity, contempt, and scorn.

Reason, Observation, and Experience—the Holy Trinity of Science—have taught us that happiness is the only good, that the time to be happy is now, and the way to be happy is to make others so. This is enough for us. In this belief we are content to live and die. If by any possibility the existence of a power superior to, and independent of, nature shall be demonstrated, there will be time enough to kneel. Until then, let us stand erect.

Notwithstanding the fact that infidels in all ages have battled for the rights of man, and have at all times been the fearless advocates of liberty and justice, we are constantly charged by the church with tearing down without building again. The church should by this time know that it is utterly impossible to rob men of their opinions. The history of religious persecution fully establishes the fact that the mind necessarily resists and defies every attempt to control it by violence. The mind necessarily clings to old ideas until prepared for the new. The moment we comprehend the truth, all erroneous ideas are of necessity cast aside.

A surgeon once called upon a poor cripple and kindly offered to render him any assistance in his power. The surgeon began to discourse very learnedly upon the nature and origin of disease; of the curative properties of certain medicines; of the advantages of exercise, air, and light; and of the various ways in which health and strength could be restored. These remarks were so full of good sense, and discovered so much profound thought and accurate knowledge, that the cripple, becoming thoroughly alarmed, cried out, "Do not, I pray you, take away my crutches. They are my only support, and without them I should be miserable indeed!" "I am not going," said the surgeon, "to take away your crutches. I am going to cure you, and then you will throw the crutches away yourself."

For the vagaries of the clouds the infidels propose to substitute the realities of earth; for superstition, the splendid demonstrations and achievements of science; and for theological tyranny, the chainless liberty of thought.

We do not say that we have discovered all; that our doctrines are the all in all of truth. We know of no end to the development of man. We cannot unravel the infinite complications of matter and force. The history of one monad is as unknown as that of the universe; one drop of water is as wonderful as all the seas;

one leaf, as all the forests; and one grain of sand, as all the stars.

We are not endeavoring to change the future, but to free the present. We are not forging fetters for our children, but we are breaking those our fathers made for us. We are the advocates of inquiry, of investigation and thought. This of itself is an admission that we are not perfectly satisfied with all our conclusions. Philosophy has not the egotism of faith. While superstition builds walls and creates obstructions, science opens all the highways of thought. We do not pretend to have circumnavigated everything, and to have solved all difficulties, but we do believe that it is better to love men than to fear gods; that it is grander and nobler to think and investigate for yourself than to repeat a creed. We are satisfied that there can be but little liberty on earth while men worship a tyrant in heaven. We do not expect to accomplish everything in our day; but we want to do what good we can, and to render all the service possible in the holy cause of human progress. We know that doing away with gods and supernatural persons and powers is not an end. It is a means to an end: the real end being the happiness of man.

Felling forests is not the end of agriculture. Driving pirates from the sea is not all there is of commerce.

We are laying the foundations of the grand temple of the future—not the temple of all the gods, but of all the people— wherein, with appropriate rites, will be celebrated the religion of Humanity. We are doing what little we can to hasten the coming of the day when society shall cease producing millionaires and mendicants—gorged indolence and famished industry—truth in rags, and superstition robed and crowned. We are looking for the time when the useful shall be the honorable; and when REASON, throned upon the world's brain, shall be the King of Kings, and God of Gods.

THOMAS PAINE

THOMAS PAINE

WITH HIS NAME LEFT OUT,
THE HISTORY OF LIBERTY CANNOT BE WRITTEN

To speak the praises of the brave and thoughtful dead, is to me a labor of gratitude and love.

Through all the centuries gone, the mind of man has been beleaguered by the mailed hosts of superstition. Slowly and painfully has advanced the army of deliverance. Hated by those they wished to rescue, despised by those they were dying to save, these grand soldiers, these immortal deliverers, have fought without thanks, labored without applause, suffered without pity, and they have died execrated and abhorred. For the good of mankind they accepted isolation, poverty, and calumny. They gave up all, sacrificed all, lost all but truth and self-respect.

One of the bravest soldiers in this army was Thomas Paine; and for one, I feel indebted to him for the liberty we are enjoying this day. Born among the poor, where children are burdens; in a country where real liberty was unknown; where the privileges of class were guarded with infinite jealousy, and the rights of the individual trampled beneath the feet of priests and nobles; where to advocate justice was treason; where intellectual freedom was

Infidelity, it is wonderful that the idea of true liberty ever entered his brain.

Poverty was his mother—Necessity his master.

He had more brains than books; more sense than education; more courage than politeness; more strength than polish. He had no veneration for old mistakes—no admiration for ancient lies. He loved the truth for the truth's sake, and for man's sake. He saw oppression on every hand; injustice everywhere; hypocrisy at the altar, venality on the bench, tyranny on the throne; and with a splendid courage he espoused the cause of the weak against the strong—of the enslaved many against the titled few.

In England he was nothing. He belonged to the lower classes. There was no avenue open for him. The people hugged their chains, and the whole power of the government was ready to crush any man who endeavored to strike a blow for the right.

At the age of thirty-seven, Thomas Paine left England for America, with the high hope of being instrumental in the establishment of a free government. In his own country he could accomplish nothing. Those two vultures—Church and State—were ready to tear in pieces and devour the heart of any one who might deny their divine right to enslave the world.

Upon his arrival in this country, he found himself possessed of a letter of introduction, signed by another Infidel, the illustrious Franklin. This, and his native genius, constituted his entire capital; and he needed no more. He found the colonies clamoring for justice; whining about their grievances; upon their knees at the foot of the throne, imploring that mixture of idiocy and insanity, George the III, by the grace of God, for a restoration of their ancient privileges. They were not endeavoring to become free men, but were trying to soften the heart of their master. They were perfectly willing to make brick if Pharaoh would furnish the straw. The colonists wished for, hoped for, and prayed for reconciliation. They did not dream of independence.

Paine gave to the world his "COMMON SENSE." It was the first argument for separation, the first assault upon the British *form* of government, the first blow for a republic, and it aroused our fathers like a trumpet's blast.

He was the first to perceive the destiny of the New World.

No other pamphlet ever accomplished such wonderful results. It was filled with argument, reason, persuasion, and unanswerable logic. It opened a new world. It filled the present with hope and the future with honor. Everywhere the people responded, and in a few months the Continental Congress declared the colonies free and independent States.

A new nation was born.

It is simple justice to say that Paine did more to cause the Declaration of Independence than any other man. Neither should it be forgotten that his attacks upon Great Britain were also attacks upon monarchy; and while he convinced the people that the colonies ought to separate from the mother country, he also proved to them that a free government is the best that can be instituted among men.

In my judgment, Thomas Paine was the best political writer that ever lived. "What he wrote was pure nature, and his soul and his pen ever went together." Ceremony, pageantry, and all the paraphernalia of power, had no effect upon him. He examined into the why and wherefore of things. He was perfectly radical in his mode of thought. Nothing short of the bedrock satisfied him. His enthusiasm for what he believed to be right knew no bounds. During all the dark scenes of the Revolution, never for one moment did he despair. Year after year his brave words were ringing through the land, and by the bivouac fires the weary soldiers read the inspiring words of "Common Sense," filled with ideas sharper than their swords, and consecrated themselves anew to the cause of Freedom.

Paine was not content with having aroused the spirit of independence, but he gave every energy of his soul to keep that spirit alive. He was with the army. He shared its defeats, its dangers, and its glory. when the situation became desperate, when gloom settled upon all, he gave them the "CRISIS." It was a cloud by day and a pillar of fire by night, leading the way to freedom, honor, and glory, He shouted to them, "These are the times that try men's souls. The summer soldier, and the sunshine patriot, will, in this crisis, shrink from the service of his country; but he that stands it now deserves the love and thanks of man and woman."

To those who wished to put the war off to some future day, with a lofty and touching spirit of self-sacrifice he said: "Every generous parent should say, 'If there must be war let it be in my day, that my child should have peace.' " To the cry that Americans were rebels, he replied: "He that rebels against reason is a real rebel; but he that in defense of reason rebels against tyranny has a better title to 'Defender of the Faith' than George the Third."

Some said it was not to the interest of the colonies to be free. Paine answered this by saying, "To know whether it be the interest of the continent to be independent, we need ask only this simple, easy question: 'Is it the interest of a man to be a boy all his life?' " He found many who would listen to nothing, and to them he said, "That to argue with a man who has renounced his reason is like giving medicine to the dead." This sentiment ought to adorn the walls of every orthodox church.

There is a world of political wisdom in this: "England lost her liberty in a long chain of right reasoning from wrong principles"; and there is real discrimination in saying, "The Greeks and Romans were strongly possessed of the spirit of liberty, but not the principles, for at the time that they were determined not to be slaves themselves, they employed their power to enslave the rest of mankind."

In his letter to the British people, in which he tried to convince them that war was not to their interest, occurs the following passage brimful of common sense: "War never can be the interest of a trading nation any more than quarreling can be profitable to a man in business. But to make war with those who trade with us is like setting a bulldog upon a customer at the shop door."

The writings of Paine fairly glitter with simple, compact, logical statements, that carry conviction to the dullest and most prejudiced. He had the happiest possible way of putting the case; in asking questions in such a way that they answer themselves; and in stating his premises so clearly that the deduction could not be avoided.

Day and night he labored for America; month after month, year after year, he gave himself to the Great Cause, until there was "a government of the people and for the people," and until the banner of stars floated over a continent redeemed, and consecrated to the happiness of mankind.

At the close of the Revolution, no one stood higher in America than Thomas Paine. The best, the wisest, the most patriotic, were his friends and admirers; and had he been thinking only of his own good he might have rested from his toils and spent the remainder of his life in comfort and ease. He could have been what the world is pleased to call "respectable." He could have died surrounded by clergymen, warriors, and statesmen. At his death there would have been an imposing funeral, miles of carriages, civic societies, salvos of artillery, a nation in mourning, and, above all, a splendid monument covered with lies.

He chose rather to benefit mankind.

At that time the seeds sown by the great Infidels were beginning to bear fruit in France. The people were beginning to think.

The eighteenth century was crowning its gray hairs with the wreath of Progress.

On every hand Science was bearing testimony against the Church. Voltaire had filled Europe with light; D'Holbach was giving to the *élite* of Paris the principles contained in his "System of Nature." The Encyclopedists had attacked superstition with information for the masses. The foundation of things began to be examined. A few had the courage to keep their shoes on and let the bush burn. Miracles began to get scarce. Everywhere the people began to inquire. America had set an example to the world. The word Liberty was in the mouths of men, and they began to wipe the dust from their knees.

The dawn of a new day had appeared.

Thomas Paine went to France. Into the new movement he threw all his energies. His fame had gone before him, and he was welcomed as a friend of the human race, and as a champion of free government.

He had never relinquished his intention of pointing out to his countrymen the defects, absurdities, and abuses of the English government. For this purpose he composed and published his greatest political work, "THE RIGHTS OF MAN." This work should be read by every man and woman. It is concise, accurate, natural, convincing, and unanswerable. It shows great thought, an intimate knowledge of the various forms of government, deep insight into the very springs of human action, and a courage that compels respect and admiration. The most difficult political problems are solved in a few sentences. The venerable arguments in favor of wrong are refuted with a question—answered with a word. For forcible illustration, apt comparison, accuracy and clearness of statement, and absolute thoroughness, it has never been excelled.

The fears of the administration were aroused, and Paine was prosecuted for libel and found guilty; and yet there is not a sentiment in the entire work that will not challenge the admiration of every civilized man. It is a magazine of political wisdom, an arsenal of ideas, and an honor, not only to Thomas Paine, but to human nature itself. It could have been written only by the man who had the generosity, the exalted patriotism, the goodness to say, "The world is my country, and to do good my religion."

There is in all the utterances of the world no grander, no sublimer sentiment. There is no creed that can be compared with it for a moment. It should be wrought in gold, adorned with jewels, and impressed upon every human heart: "The world is my country, and to do good my religion."

In 1792, Paine was elected by the department of Calais as their representative in the National Assembly. So great was his popularity in France that he was selected about the same time by the people of no less than four departments.

Upon taking his place in the Assembly he was appointed as one of a committee to draft a constitution for France. Had the French people taken the advice of Thomas Paine there would have been no "reign of terror." The streets of Paris would not have been filled with blood. The Revolution would have been the grandest success of the world. The truth is that Paine was too conservative to suit the leaders of the French Revolution. They, to a great extent, were carried away by hatred, and a desire to destroy. They had suffered so long, they had borne so much, that it was impossible for them to be moderate in the hour of victory.

Besides all this, the French people had been so robbed by the government, so degraded by the church, that they were not fit material with which to construct a republic. Many of the leaders longed to establish a beneficent and just government, but the people asked for revenge.

Paine was filled with a real love for mankind. His philanthropy was boundless. He wished to destroy monarchy—not the monarch. He voted for the destruction of tyranny, and against the death of the king. He wished to establish a government on a new basis; one that would forget the past; one that would give privileges to none, and protection to all.

In the Assembly, where nearly all were demanding the execution of the king—where to differ from the majority was to be suspected, and where to be suspected was almost certain death— Thomas Paine had the courage, the goodness, and the justice to vote against death. To vote against the execution of the king was a vote against his own life. This was the sublimity of devotion to principle. For this he was arrested, imprisoned, and doomed to death.

Search the records of the world and you will find but few sublimer acts than that of Thomas Paine voting against the king's death. He, the hater of despotism, the abhorrer of monarchy, the champion of the rights of man, the republican, accepting death to save the life of a deposed tyrant—of a throneless king. This was the last grand act of his political life—the sublime conclusion of his political career.

All his life he had been the disinterested friend of man. He had labored—not for money, not for fame, but for the general good. He had aspired to no office, had asked no recognition of his services, but had ever been content to labor as a common soldier in the army of Progress. Confining his efforts to no country, looking upon the world as his field of action, filled with a genuine love for the right, he found himself imprisoned by the very people he had striven to save.

Had his enemies succeeded in bringing him to the block, he would have escaped the calumnies and the hatred of the Christian world. In this country, at least, he would have ranked with the proudest names. On the anniversary of the Declaration his name would have been upon the lips of all the orators, and his memory in the hearts of all the people.

Thomas Paine had not finished his career.

He had spent his life thus far in destroying the power of kings, and now he turned his attention to the priests. He knew that every abuse had been embalmed in Scripture—that every outrage was in partnership with some holy text. He knew that the throne skulked behind the altar, and both behind a pretended revelation from God. By this time he had found that it was of little use to free the body and leave the mind in chains. He had explored the foundations of despotism, and had found them infinitely rotten. He had dug under the throne, and it occurred to him that he would take a look behind the altar.

The result of his investigations was given to the world in the "AGE OF REASON." From the moment of its publication he became infamous. He was calumniated beyond measure. To slander him was to secure the thanks of the church. All his services were instantly forgotten, disparaged, or denied. He was shunned as though he had been a pestilence. Most of his old friends forsook him. He was regarded as a moral plague, and at the bare mention of his name the bloody hands of the church were raised in horror. He was denounced as the most despicable of men.

Not content with following him to his grave, they pursued him after death with redoubled fury, and recounted with infinite gusto and satisfaction the supposed horrors of his deathbed, gloried in the fact that he was forlorn and friendless, and gloated like fiends over what they supposed to be the agonizing remorse of his lonely death.

It is wonderful that all his services were thus forgotten. It is amazing that one kind word did not fall from some pulpit; that some one did not accord to him, at least—honesty. Strange, that in the general denunciation some one did not remember his labor for liberty, his devotion to principle, his zeal for the rights of his fellowmen. He had, by brave and splendid effort, associated his name with the cause of Progress. He had made it impossible to write the history of political freedom with his name left out. He was one of the creators of light; one of the heralds of the dawn. He hated tyranny in the name of kings, and in the name of God, with every drop of his noble blood. He believed in liberty and justice, and in the sacred doctrine of human equality. Under these divine banners he fought the battle of his life. In both worlds he offered his blood for the good of man. In the wilderness of America, in the French Assembly, in the somber cell waiting for death, he was the same unflinching, unwavering friend of his race; the same undaunted champion of universal freedom. And for this he has been hated; for this the church has violated even his grave.

This is enough to make one believe that nothing is more natural than for men to devour their benefactors. The people in all ages have been crucified and glorified. Whoever lifts his voice against abuses, whoever arraigns the past at the bar of the present, whoever asks the king to show his commission, or questions the authority of the priest, will be denounced as the enemy of man and God. In all ages reason has been regarded as the enemy of religion. Nothing has been considered so pleasing to the Deity as a total denial of the authority of your own mind. Self-reliance has been thought a deadly sin; and the idea of living and dying without the aid and consolation of superstition has always horrified the church. By some unaccountable infatuation, belief has been and still is considered of immense importance. All religions have been based upon the idea that God will forever reward the true believer, and eternally damn the man who doubts or denies. Belief is regarded as the one essential thing. To practice justice, to love mercy, is not enough. You must believe in some incomprehensible creed. You must say, "Once one is three, and three times one is one." The man who practiced every virtue, but failed to believe, was execrated. Nothing so outrages the feelings of the church as a moral unbeliever—nothing so horrible as a charitable atheist.

When Paine was born, the world was religious, the pulpit was the real throne, and the churches were making every effort to crush out of the brain the idea that it had the right to think.

The splendid saying of Lord Bacon, that "the inquiry of truth, which is the love-making or wooing of it, the knowledge of truth, which is the presence of it, and the belief of truth, which is the enjoying of it, are the sovereign good of human nature," has been, and ever will be, rejected by religionists. Intellectual liberty, as a matter of necessity, forever destroys the idea that belief is either praise- or blameworthy, and is wholly inconsistent with every creed in Christendom. Paine recognized this truth. He also saw that as long as the Bible was considered inspired, this infamous doctrine of the virtue of belief would be believed and preached. He examined the Scriptures for himself, and found them filled with cruelty, absurdity, and immorality.

He made up his mind to sacrifice himself for the good of his fellowmen.

He commenced with the assertion, "That any system of religion that has anything in it that shocks the mind of a child cannot be a true system." What a beautiful, what a tender sentiment! No wonder the church began to hate him. He believed in one God, and no more. After this life he hoped for happiness. He believed that true religion consisted in doing justice, loving mercy, in endeavoring to make our fellow creatures happy, and in offering to God the fruit of the heart. He denied the inspiration of the Scriptures. This was his crime.

He contended that it is a contradiction in terms to call anything a revelation that comes to us second-hand, either verbally or in writing. He asserted that revelation is necessarily limited to the first communication, and that after that it is only an account of something which another person says was a revelation to him. We have only his word for it, as it was never made to us. This argument never has and probably never will be answered. He denied the divine origin of Christ, and showed conclusively that the pretended prophecies of the Old Testament had no reference to him whatever; and yet he believed that Christ was a virtuous and amiable man, that the morality he taught and practiced was of the most benevolent and elevated character, and that it had not been exceeded by any. Upon this point he entertained the same sentiments now held by the Unitarians, and in fact by all the most enlightened Christians.

In his time the church believed and taught that every word in the Bible was absolutely true. Since his day it has been proven false in its cosmogony, false in its astronomy, false in its chronology, false in its history, and so far as the Old Testament is concerned, false in almost everything. There are but few, if any, scientific men who apprehend that the Bible is literally true. Who on earth at this day would pretend to settle any scientific question by a text from the Bible? The old belief is confined to the ignorant and zealous. The church itself will before long be driven to occupy the position of Thomas Paine. The best minds of the orthodox world, today, are endeavoring to prove the existence of a personal Deity. All other questions occupy a minor place. You are no longer asked to swallow the Bible whole, whale, Jonah, and all; you are simply required to believe in God, and pay your pew rent. There is not now an enlightened minister in the world who will seriously contend that Samson's strength was in his hair, or that the necromancers of Egypt could turn water into blood and pieces of wood into serpents. These follies have passed away, and the only reason that the religious world can now have for disliking Paine is that they have been forced to adopt so many of his opinions.

Paine thought the barbarities of the Old Testament inconsistent with what he deemed the real character of God. He believed that murder, massacre, and indiscriminate slaughter had never been

commanded by the Deity. He regarded much of the Bible as childish, unimportant, and foolish. The scientific world entertains the
same opinion. Paine attacked the Bible precisely in the same spirit
in which he had attacked the pretensions of kings. He used the
same weapons. All the pomp in the world could not make him
cower. His reason knew no "Holy of Holies," except the abode
of Truth. The sciences were then in their infancy. The attention
of the really learned had not been directed to an impartial ex-
amination of our pretended revelation. It was accepted by most
as a matter of course. The church was all-powerful, and no one,
unless thoroughly imbued with the spirit of self-sacrifice, thought
for a moment of disputing the fundamental doctrines of Christianity. The infamous doctrines that salvation depends upon belief—upon a mere intellectual conviction—was then believed and
preached. To doubt was to secure the damnation of your soul.
This absurd and devilish doctrine shocked the common sense of
Thomas Paine, and he denounced it with the fervor of honest
indignation. This doctrine, although infinitely ridiculous, has been
nearly universal, and has been as hurtful as senseless. For the
overthrow of this infamous tenet, Paine exerted all his strength.
He left few arguments to be used by those who should come
after him, and he used none that have been refuted. The combined
wisdom and genius of all mankind cannot possibly conceive of
an argument against liberty of thought. Neither can they show
why any one should be punished, either in this world or another,
for acting honestly in accordance with reason; and yet a doctrine
with every possible argument against it has been, and still is, believed
and defended by the entire orthodox world. Can it be possible
that we have been endowed with reason simply that our souls
may be caught in its toils and snares, that we may be led by
its false and delusive glare out of the narrow path that leads to
joy into the broad way of everlasting death? Is it possible that
we have been given reason simply that we may through faith ignore
its deductions, and avoid its conclusions? Ought the sailor to throw
away his compass and depend entirely upon the fog? If reason

is not to be depended upon in matters of religion, that is to say, in respect of our duties to the Deity, why should it be relied upon in matters respecting the rights of our fellows? Why should we throw away the laws given to Moses by God himself, and have the audacity to make some of our own? How dare we drown the thunders of Sinai by calling the ayes and noes in a petty legislature? If reason can determine what is merciful, what is just, the duties of man to man, what more do we want either in time or eternity?

Down, forever down, with any religion that requires upon its ignorant altar the sacrifice of the goddess Reason, that compels her to abdicate forever the shining throne of the soul, strips from her form the imperial purple, snatches from her hand the scepter of thought and makes her the bondwoman of a senseless faith!

If a man should tell you that he had the most beautiful painting in the world, and after taking you where it was should insist upon having your eyes shut, you would likely suspect either that he had no painting or that it was some pitiable daub. Should he tell you that he was a most excellent performer on the violin, and yet refuse to play unless your ears were stopped, you would think, to say the least of it, that he had an odd way of convincing you of his musical ability. But would his conduct be any more wonderful than that of a religionist who asks that before examining his creed you will have the kindness to throw away your reason? The first gentleman says, "Keep your eyes shut, my picture will bear everything but being seen;" "Keep your ears stopped, my music objects to nothing but being heard." The last says, "Away with your reason, my religion dreads nothing but being understood."

So far as I am concerned, I most cheerfully admit that most Christians are honest, and most ministers sincere. We do not attack them; we attack their creed. We accord to them the same rights that we ask for ourselves. We believe that their doctrines are hurtful. We believe that the frightful text, "He that believes shall be saved and he that believeth not shall be damned," has covered the earth with blood. It has filled the heart with arrogance, cruelty, and murder. It has caused the religious wars; bound hundreds of thousands to the stake; founded inquisitions; filled dungeons; invented instruments of torture; taught the mother to hate her child; imprisoned the mind; filled the world with ignorance; persecuted the lovers of wisdom; built the monasteries and convents; made happiness a crime, investigation a sin, and self-reliance a blasphemy. It has poisoned the springs of learning; misdirected the energies of the world; filled all countries with want; housed the people in hovels; fed them with famine; and but for the efforts of a few brave Infidels it would have taken the world back to the midnight of barbarism, and left the heavens without a star.

The maligners of Paine say that he had no right to attack this doctrine, because he was unacquainted with the dead languages; and for this reason, it was a piece of pure impudence in him to investigate the Scriptures.

Is it necessary to understand Hebrew in order to know that cruelty is not a virtue, that murder is inconsistent with infinite goodness, and that eternal punishment can be inflicted upon man only by an eternal fiend? Is it really essential to conjugate the Greek verbs before you can make up your mind as to the probability of dead people getting out of their graves? Must one be versed in Latin before he is entitled to express his opinion as to the genuineness of a pretended revelation from God? Common sense belongs exclusively to no tongue. Logic is not confined to, nor has it been buried with, the dead languages. Paine attacked the Bible as it is translated. If the translation is wrong, let its defenders correct it.

The Christianity of Paine's day is not the Christianity of our time. There has been a great improvement since then. One hundred and fifty years ago the foremost preachers of our time would have perished at the stake. A Universalist would have been torn in pieces in England, Scotland, and America. Unitarians would have found themselves in the stocks, pelted by the rabble with dead cats, after which their ears would have been cut off, their tongues bored, and their foreheads branded. Less than one hundred and fifty years ago the following law was in force in Maryland:

Be it enacted by the Right Honorable, the Lord Proprietor, by and with the advice and consent of his Lordship's governor, and the upper and lower houses of the Assembly, and the authority of the same:

That if any person shall hereafter, within this province, wittingly, maliciously, and advisedly, by writing or speaking, blaspheme or curse God, or deny our Savior, Jesus Christ, to be the Son of God, or shall deny the Holy Trinity, the Father, Son, and Holy Ghost, or the Godhead of any of the three persons, or the unity of the Godhead, or shall utter any profane words concerning the Holy Trinity, or any of the persons thereof, and shall thereof be convict by verdict, shall, for the first offense, be bored through the tongue, and fined twenty pounds to be levied of his body. And for the second offense, the offender shall be stigmatized by burning in the forehead with the letter B, and fined forty pounds. And that for the third offense the offender shall suffer death without the benefit of clergy.

The strange thing about this law is that it has never been repealed, and is still in force in the District of Columbia. Laws like this were in force in most of the colonies, and in all countries where the church had power.

In the Old Testament, the death penalty was attached to hundreds of offenses. It has been the same in all Christian countries. Today, in civilized governments, the death penalty is attached only to murder and treason; and in some it has been entirely abolished. What a commentary upon the divine systems of the world!

In the day of Thomas Paine, the church was ignorant, bloody, and relentless. In Scotland the "Kirk" was at the summit of its power. It was a full sister of the Spanish Inquisition. It waged war upon human nature. It was the enemy of happiness, the hater of joy, and the despiser of religious liberty. It taught parents to murder their children rather than allow them to propagate error. If the mother held opinions of which the infamous "Kirk" disapproved, her children were taken from her arms, her babe from her very bosom, and she was not allowed to see them or to write them a word. It would not allow shipwrecked sailors to be rescued from drowning on Sunday. It sought to annihilate pleasure, to pollute the heart by filling it with religious cruelty and gloom, and to change mankind into a vast horde of pious, heartless fiends. One of the most famous Scotch divines said: "The Kirk holds that religious toleration is not far from blasphemy." And this same Scotch Kirk denounced, beyond measure, the man who had the moral grandeur to say, "The world is my country, and to do good my religion." And this same Kirk abhorred the man who said, "Any system of religion that shocks the mind of a child cannot be a true system."

At that time nothing so delighted the church as the beauties of endless torment, and listening to the weak wailings of damned infants struggling in the slimy coils and poison folds of the worm that never dies.

About the beginning of the nineteenth century, a boy by the name of Thomas Aikenhead was indicted and tried at Edinburgh for having denied the inspiration of the Scriptures, and for having, on several occasions, when cold, wished himself in hell that he might get warm. Notwithstanding the poor boy recanted and begged for mercy, he was found guilty and hanged. His body was thrown in a hole at the foot of the scaffold and covered with stones.

Prosecutions and executions like this were common in every Christian country, and all of them were based upon the belief that an intellectual conviction is a crime.

No wonder the church hated and traduced the author of the "Age of Reason."

England was filled with Puritan gloom and Episcopal ceremony. All religious conceptions were of the grossest nature. The ideas of crazy fanatics and extravagant poets were taken as sober facts. Milton had clothed Christianity in the soiled and faded finery of the gods—had added to the story of Christ the fables of mythology. He gave to the Protestant Church the most outrageously material ideas of the Deity. He turned all the angels into soldiers—made heaven a battlefield, put Christ in uniform, and described God as a militia general. His works were considered by the Protestants nearly as sacred as the Bible itself, and the imagination of the people was thoroughly polluted by the horrible imagery, the sublime absurdity of the blind Milton.

Heaven and hell were realities—the judgment day was expected—books of account would be opened. Every man would hear the charges against him read. God was supposed to sit on a golden throne, surrounded by the tallest angels, with harps in their hands and crowns on their heads. The goats would be thrust into eternal fire on the left, while the orthodox sheep, on the right, were to gambol on sunny slopes forever and forever.

The nation was profoundly ignorant, and consequently extremely religious, so far as belief was concerned.

In Europe, Liberty was lying chained in the Inquisition—her white bosom stained with blood. In the New World the Puritans had been hanging and burning in the name of God, and selling white Quaker children into slavery in the name of Christ, who said, "Suffer little children to come unto me."

Under such conditions progress was impossible. Some one had to lead the way. The church is, and always has been, incapable of a forward movement. Religion always looks back. The church has already reduced Spain to a guitar, Italy to a hand organ, and Ireland to exile.

Some one not connected with the church had to attack the monster that was eating out the heart of the world. Some one had to sacrifice himself for the good of all. The people were in the most abject slavery; their manhood had been taken from them by pomp, by pageantry and power. Progress is born of doubt and inquiry.

The church never doubts—never inquires. To doubt is heresy—to inquire is to admit that you do not know—the church does neither.

More than a century ago Catholicism, wrapped in robes red with the innocent blood of millions, holding in her frantic clutch crowns and scepters, honors and gold, the keys of heaven and hell, trampling beneath her feet the liberties of nation, in the proud moment of almost universal dominion, felt within her heartless breast the deadly dagger of Voltaire. From that blow the church never can recover. Livid with hatred she launched her eternal anathema at the great destroyer, and ignorant Protestants have echoed the curse of Rome.

In our country the church was all-powerful, and although divided into many sects, would instantly unite to repel a common foe.

Paine struck the first grand blow.

The "Age of Reason" did more to undermine the power of the Protestant Church than all other books then known. It furnished an immense amount of food for thought. It was written for the average mind, and is a straightforward, honest investigation of the Bible, and of the Christian system.

Paine did not falter, from the first page to the last. He gives you his candid thought, and candid thoughts are always valuable.

The "Age of Reason" has liberalized us all. It put arguments in the mouths of the people; it put the church on the defensive; it enabled somebody in every village to corner the parson; it made the world wiser, and the church better; it took power from the pulpit and divided it among the pews.

Just in proportion that the human race has advanced, the church has lost power. There is no exception to this rule.

No nation ever materially advanced that held strictly to the religion of its founders.

No nation ever gave itself wholly to the control of the church without losing its power, its honor, and existence.

Every church pretends to have found the exact truth. This is the end of progress. Why pursue that which you have? Why investigate when you know?

Every creed is a rock in running water: humanity sweeps by it. Every creed cries to the universe, "Halt!" A creed is the ignorant Past bullying the enlightened Present.

The ignorant are not satisfied with what can be demonstrated. Science is too slow for them, and so they invent creeds. They demand completeness. A sublime segment, a grand fragment, are of no value to them. They demand the complete circle—the entire structure.

In music they want a melody with a recurring accent at measured periods. In religion they insist upon immediate answers to the questions of creation and destiny. The alpha and omega of all things must be in the alphabet of their superstition. A religion that cannot answer every question, and guess every conundrum is, in their estimation, worse than worthless. They desire a kind of theological dictionary—a religious ready reckoner, together with guideboards at all crossings and turns. They mistake impudence for authority, solemnity for wisdom, and bathos for inspiration. The beginning and the end are what they demand. The grand flight of the eagle is nothing to them. They want the nest in which he was hatched, and especially the dry limb upon which he roosts. Anything that can be learned is hardly worth knowing. The present is considered of no value in itself. Happiness must not be expected this side of the clouds, and can only be attained by self-denial and faith; not self-denial for the good of others, but for the salvation of your own sweet self.

Paine denied the authority of bibles and creeds; this was his crime, and for this the world shut the door in his face, and emptied its slops upon him from the windows.

I challenge the world to show that Thomas Paine ever wrote one line, one word in favor of tyranny—in favor of immorality; one line, one word against what he believed to be for the highest and best interest of mankind; one line, one word against justice, charity, or liberty, and yet he has been pursued as though he had been a fiend from hell. His memory has been execrated as though he had murdered some Uriah for his wife; driven some Hagar into the desert to starve with his child upon her bosom; defiled his own daughters; ripped open with the sword the sweet bodies of loving and innocent women; advised one brother to assassinate another; kept a harem with seven hundred wives and three hundred concubines; or had persecuted Christians even unto strange cities.

The church has pursued Paine to deter others. No effort has been in any age of the world spared to crush out opposition. The church used painting, music, and architecture simply to degrade mankind. But there are men that nothing can awe. There have been at all times brave spirits that dared even the gods. Some proud head has always been above the waves. In every age some Diogenes has sacrificed to all the gods. True genius never cowers, and there is always some Samson feeling for the pillars of authority.

Cathedrals and domes, and chimes and chants—temples frescoed and groined and carved, and gilded with gold—altars and tapers, and paintings of virgin and babe—censor and chalice—chasuble, paten, and alb—organs and anthems and incense rising to the winged and blest—maniple, amice, and stole—crosses and crosiers, tiaras and crowns—miters and missals and masses—rosaries, relics, and robes—martyrs and saints, and windows stained as with the blood of Christ—never, never for one moment awed the brave, proud spirit of the Infidel. He knew that all the pomp and glitter had been purchased with Liberty—that priceless jewel of the soul. In looking at the cathedral he remembered the dungeon. The music of the organ was not loud enough to drown the clank of fetters. He could not forget that the taper had lighted the fagot. He knew that the cross adorned the hilt of the sword, and so where others worshiped, he wept and scorned.

The doubter, the investigator, the Infidel have been the saviors of liberty. This truth is beginning to be realized, and the truly intellectual are honoring the brave thinkers of the past.

But the church is as unforgiving as ever, and still wonders why any Infidel should be wicked enough to endeavor to destroy her power.

I will tell the church why.

You have imprisoned the human mind; you have been the enemy of liberty; you have burned us at the stake—wasted us upon slow fires—torn our flesh with iron; you have covered us with chains—treated us as outcasts; you have filled the world with fear; you have taken our wives and children from our arms; you have confiscated our property; you have denied us the right to testify in courts of justice; you have branded us with infamy; you have torn out our tongues; you have refused us burial. In the name of your religion, you have robbed us of every right; and after having inflicted upon us every evil that can be inflicted in this world, you have fallen upon your knees, and with clasped hands implored your God to torment us forever.

Can you wonder that we hate your doctrines—that we despise your creeds—that we feel proud to know that we are beyond your power—that we are free in spite of you—that we can express our honest thought, and that the whole world is grandly rising into the blessed light?

Can you wonder that we point with pride to the fact that Infidelity has ever been found battling for the rights of man, for the liberty of conscience, and for the happiness of all?

Can you wonder that we are proud to know that we have always been disciples of Reason, and soldiers of Freedom; that we have denounced tyranny and superstition, and have kept our hands unstained with human blood?

We deny that religion is the end of object of this life. When it is so considered it becomes destructive of happiness—the real end of life. It becomes a hydra-headed monster, reaching in terrible coils from the heavens, and thrusting its thousand fangs into the bleeding, quivering hearts of men. It devours their substance, builds palaces for God (who dwells not in temples made with hands), and allows his children to die in huts and hovels. It fills the earth with mourning, heaven with hatred, the present with fear, and all the future with despair.

Virtue is a subordination of the passions to the intellect. It is to act in accordance with your highest convictions. It does not consist in believing, but in doing. This is the sublime truth that the Infidels of all ages have uttered. They have handed the torch from one to the other through all the years that have fled. Upon the altar of Reason they have kept the sacred fire, and through the long midnight of faith they fed the divine flame.

Infidelity is liberty; all religion is slavery. In every creed man is the slave of God—woman is the slave of man and the sweet children are the slaves of all.

We do not want creeds; we want knowledge—we want happiness.

And yet we are told by the church that we have accomplished nothing; that we are simply destroyers; that we tear down without building again.

Is it nothing to free the mind? Is it nothing to civilize mankind? Is it nothing to fill the world with light, with discovery, with science? Is it nothing to dignify man and exalt the intellect? Is it nothing to grope your way into the dreary prisons, the damp and dropping dungeons, the dark and silent cells of superstition, where the souls of men are chained to floors of stone; to greet them like a ray of light, like the song of a bird, the murmur of a stream; to see the dull eyes open and grow slowly bright; to feel yourself grasped by the shrunken and unused hands, and hear yourself thanked by a strange and hollow voice?

Is it nothing to conduct these souls gradually into the blessed light of day—to let them see again the happy fields, the sweet, green earth, and hear the everlasting music of the waves? Is it nothing to make men wipe the dust from their swollen knees, the tears from their blanched and furrowed cheeks? Is it a small thing to reave the heavens of an insatiate monster and write upon the eternal dome, glittering with stars, the grand word—FREEDOM?

Is it a small thing to quench the flames of hell with the holy tears of pity—to unbind the martyr from the stake—break all the chains—put out the fires of civil war—stay the sword of the fanatic, and tear the bloody hands of the Church from the white throat of Science?

Is it a small thing to make men truly free—to destroy the dogmas of ignorance, prejudice, and power—the poisoned fables of superstition, and drive from the beautiful face of the earth the fiend of Fear?

It does seem as though the most zealous Christian must at

times entertain some doubt as to the divine origin of his religion. For eighteen hundred years the doctrine has been preached. For more than a thousand years the church had, to a great extent, the control of the civilized world, and what has been the result? Are the Christian nations patterns of charity and forbearance? On the contrary, their principal business is to destroy each other. More than five millions of Christians are trained, educated, and drilled to murder their fellow Christians. Every nation is groaning under a vast debt incurred in carrying on war against other Christians, or defending itself from Christian assault. The world is covered with forts to protect Christians from Christians, and every sea is covered with iron monsters ready to blow Christian brains into eternal froth. Millions upon millions are annually expended in the effort to construct still more deadly and terrible engines of death. Industry is crippled, honest toil is robbed, and even beggary is taxed to defray the expenses of Christian warfare. There must be some other way to reform this world. We have tried creed, and dogma and fable, and they have failed; and they have failed in all the nations' dead.

The people perish for the lack of knowledge.

Nothing but education—scientific education—can benefit mankind. We must find out the laws of nature and conform to them.

We need free bodies and free minds,—free labor and free thought,—chainless hands and fetterless brains. Free labor will give us wealth. Free thought will give us truth.

We need men with moral courage to speak and write their real thoughts, and to stand by their convictions, even to the very death. We need have no fear of being too radical. The future will verify all grand and brave predictions. Paine was splendidly in advance of his time; but he was orthodox compared with the Infidels of today.

Science, the great Iconoclast, has been busy since 1809, and by the highway of Progress are the broken images of the Past.

On every hand the people advance. The Vicar of God has

been pushed from the throne of the Caesars, and upon the roofs of the Eternal City falls once more the shadow of the Eagle.

All has been accomplished by the heroic few. The men of science have explored heaven and earth, and with infinite patience have furnished the facts. The brave thinkers have used them. The gloomy caverns of superstition have been transformed into temples of thought, and the demons of the past are the angels of today.

Science took a handful of sand, constructed a telescope, and with it explored the starry depths of heaven. Science wrested from the gods their thunderbolts; and now, the electric spark, freighted with thought and love, flashes under all the waves of the sea. Science took a tear from the cheek of unpaid labor, converted it into steam, created a giant that turns with tireless arm the countless wheels of toil.

Thomas Paine was one of the intellectual heroes—one of the men to whom we are indebted. His name is associated forever with the Great Republic. As long as free government exists he will be remembered, admired, and honored.

He lived a long, laborious, and useful life. The world is better for his having lived. For the sake of truth he accepted hatred and reproach for his portion. He ate the bitter bread of sorrow. His friends were untrue to him because he was true to himself, and true to them. He lost the respect of what is called society, but kept his own. His life is what the world calls failure and what history calls success.

If to love your fellowmen more than yourself is goodness, Thomas Paine was good.

If to be in advance of your time—to be a pioneer in the direction of right—is greatness, Thomas Paine was great.

If to avow your principles and discharge your duty in the presence of death is heroic, Thomas Paine was a hero.

At the age of seventy-three, death touched his tired heart. He died in the land his genius defended—under the flag he gave to the skies. Slander cannot touch him now—hatred cannot reach him more. He sleeps in the sanctuary of the tomb, beneath the quiet of the stars.

A few more years—a few more brave men—a few more rays of light, and mankind will venerate the memory of him who said:

"ANY SYSTEM OF RELIGION THAT SHOCKS THE MIND OF A CHILD CANNOT BE A TRUE SYSTEM";

"THE WORLD IS MY COUNTRY, AND TO DO GOOD MY RELIGION."

INDIVIDUALITY

INDIVIDUALITY

"HIS SOUL WAS LIKE A STAR AND DWELT APART"

On every hand are the enemies of individuality and mental freedom. Custom meets us at the cradle and leaves us only at the tomb. Our first questions are answered by ignorance, and our last by superstition. We are pushed and dragged by countless hands along the beaten track, and our entire training can be summed up in the word—suppression. Our desire to have a thing or to do a thing is considered as conclusive evidence that we ought not to have it, and ought not to do it. At every turn we run against cherubim and a flaming sword guarding some entrance to the Eden of our desire. We are allowed to investigate all subjects in which we feel no particular interest, and to express the opinions of the majority with the utmost freedom. We are taught that liberty of speech should never be carried to the extent of contradicting the dead witnesses of a popular superstition. Society offers continual rewards for self-betrayal, and they are nearly all earned and claimed, and some are paid.

We have all read accounts of Christian gentlemen remarking, when about to be hanged, how much better it would have been for them if they had only followed a mother's advice. But after all, how fortunate it is for the world that the maternal advice has not always been followed. How fortunate it is for us all that it is somewhat unnatural for a human being to obey. Universal obedience is universal stagnation; disobedience is one of the conditions of progress. Select any age of the world and tell me what would have been the effect of implicit obedience. Suppose the church had had absolute control of the human mind at any time, would not the words liberty and progress have been blotted from human speech? In defiance of advice, the world has advanced.

Suppose the atronomers had controlled the science of astronomy; suppose the doctors had controlled the science of medicine; suppose kings had been left to fix the forms of government; suppose our fathers had taken the advice of Paul, who said, "Be subject to the powers that be, because they are ordained of God"; suppose the church could control the world today, we would go back to chaos and old night. Philosophy would be branded as infamous; Science would again press its pale and thoughtful face against the prison bars, and round the limbs of liberty would climb the bigot's flame.

It is a blessed thing that in every age some one has had individuality enough and courage enough to stand by his own convictions,—some one who had the grandeur to say his say. I believe it was Magellan who said, "The church says the earth is flat; but I have seen its shadow on the moon, and I have more confidence even in a shadow than in the church." On the prow of his ship were disobedience, defiance, scorn, and success.

The trouble with most people is, they bow to what is called authority; they have a certain reverence for the old because it is old. They think a man is better for being dead, especially if he has been dead a long time. They think the fathers of their nation were the greatest and best of all mankind. All these things they implicitly believe because it is popular and patriotic, and because they were told so when they were very small, and remember distinctly of hearing mother read it out of a book. (It is hard to overestimate the influence of early training in the direction of superstition. You first teach children that a certain book is true—that it was written by God himself—that to question its truth is a sin, that to deny it is a crime, and that should they die without believing in that book they will be forever damned without benefit of clergy. The consequence is that long before they read that book, they believe it to be true. When they do read it their minds are wholly unfitted to investigate its claims. They accept it as a matter of course.)

In this way the reason is overcome, the sweet instincts of humanity are blotted from the heart, and while reading its infamous pages even justice throws aside her scales, shrieking for revenge, and charity, with bloody hands, applauds a deed of murder. In this way we are taught that the revenge of man is the justice of God; that mercy is not the same everywhere. In this way the ideas of our race have been subverted. In this way we have made tyrants, bigots, and inquisitors. In this way the brain of man has become a kind of palimpsest upon which, and over the writings of nature, superstition has scrawled her countless lies. One great trouble is that most teachers are dishonest. They teach as certainties those things concerning which they entertain doubts. They do not say "we *think* this is so," but "we *know* this is so." They do not appeal to the reason of the pupil, but they command his faith. They keep all doubts to themselves; they do not explain, they assert. All this is infamous. In this way you may make Christians, but you cannot make men; you cannot make women. You can make followers, but no leaders; disciples, but no Christs. You may promise power, honor, and happiness to all those who will blindly follow, but you cannot keep your promise.

A monarch said to a hermit, "Come with me and I will give you power."

"I have all the power that I know how to use," replied the hermit.

"Come," said the king, "I will give you wealth."

"I have no wants that money can supply," said the hermit.

"I will give you honor," said the monarch.

"Ah, honor cannot be given, it must be earned," was the hermit's answer.

"Come," said the king, making a last appeal, "and I will give you happiness."

"No," said the man of solitude, "there is no happiness without liberty, and he who follows cannot be free."

"You shall have liberty too," said the king.

"Then I will stay where I am," said the old man.

And all the king's courtiers thought the hermit a fool.

Now and then somebody examines, and in spite of all keeps his manhood, and has the courage to follow where his reason leads. Then the pious get together and repeat wise saws, and exchange knowing nods and most prophetic winks. The stupidly wise sit owl-like on the dead limbs of the tree of knowledge, and solemnly hoot. Wealth sneers, and fashion laughs, and respectability passes by on the other side, and scorn points with all her skinny fingers, and all the snakes of superstition writhe and hiss, and slander lends her tongue, and infamy her brand, and perjury her oath, and the law its power, and bigotry tortures, and the church kills.

The church hates a thinker precisely for the same reason a robber dislikes a sheriff, or a thief despises the prosecuting witness. Tyranny likes courtiers, flatterers, followers, fawners, and superstition wants believers, disciples, zealots, hypocrites, and subscribers. The church demands worship—the very thing that man should give to no being, human or divine. To worship another is to degrade yourself. Worship is awe and dread and vague fear and blind hope. It is the spirit of worship that elevates the one and degrades the many; that builds palaces for robbers, erects monuments to crime, and forges manacles even for its own hands. The spirit of worship is the spirit of tyranny. The worshiper always regrets that he is not the worshiped. We should all remember that the intellect has no knees, and that whatever the attitude of the body may be, the brave soul is always found erect. Whoever worships, abdicates. Whoever believes at the command of power, tramples his own individuality beneath his feet, and voluntarily robs himself of all that renders man superior to the brute.

The despotism of faith is justified upon the ground that Christian countries are the grandest and most prosperous of the world. At one time the same thing could have been truly said in India, in Egypt, in Greece, in Rome, and in every other country that has, in the history of the world, swept to empire. This argument not only proves too much, but the assumption upon which it is based is utterly false. Numberless circumstances and countless conditions have produced the prosperity of the Christian world. The truth is, we have advanced in spite of religious zeal, ignorance, and opposition. The church has won no victories for the rights of man. Luther labored to reform the church—Voltaire, to reform men. Over every fortress of tyranny has waved, and still waves, the banner of the church. Wherever brave blood has been shed, the sword of the church has been wet. On every chain has been the sign of the cross. The altar and throne have leaned against and supported each other.

All that is good in our civilization is the result of commerce, climate, soil, geographical position, industry, invention, discovery, art, and science. The church has been the enemy of progress, for the reason that it has endeavored to prevent man thinking for himself. To prevent thought is to prevent all advancement except in the direction of faith.

Who can imagine the infinite impudence of a church assuming to think for the human race? Who can imagine the infinite impudence of a church that pretends to be the mouthpiece of God, and in his name threatens to inflict eternal punishment upon those who honestly reject its claims and scorn its pretensions? By what right does a man, or an organization of men, or a god, claim to hold a brain in bondage? When a fact can be demonstrated, force is unnecessary; when it cannot be demonstrated, an appeal to force is infamous. In the presence of the unknown all have an equal right to think.

Over the vast plain, called life, we are all travelers, and not one traveler is perfectly certain that he is going in the right direction. True it is that no other plain is so well supplied with guideboards.

At every turn and crossing you will find them, and upon each one is written the exact direction and distance. One great trouble is, however, that these boards are all different, and the result is that most travelers are confused in proportion to the number they read. Thousands of people are around each of these signs, and each one is doing his best to convince the traveler that his particular board is the only one upon which the least reliance can be placed, and that if his road is taken the reward for so doing will be infinite and eternal, while all the other roads are said to lead to hell, and all the makers of the other guideboards are declared to be heretics, hypocrites, and liars. "Well," says a traveler, "you may be right in what you say, but allow me at least to read some of the other directions and examine a little into their claims. I wish to rely a little upon my own judgment in a matter of so great importance." "No, sir," shouts the zealot, "that is the very thing you are not allowed to do. You must go my way without investigation, or you are as good as damned already." "Well," says the traveler, "if that is so, I believe I had better go your way." And so most of them go along, taking the word of those who know as little as themselves. Now and then comes one who, in spite of all threats, calmly examines the claims of all, and as calmly rejects them all. These travelers take roads of their own, and are denounced by all the others as infidels and atheists.

Around all of these guideboards, as far as the eye can reach, the ground is covered with mountains of human bones, crumbling and bleaching in the rain and sun. They are the bones of murdered men and women—fathers, mothers, and babes.

In my judgment, every human being should take a road of his own. Every mind should be true to itself—should think, investigate, and conclude for itself. This is a duty alike incumbent upon pauper and prince. Every soul should repel dictation and tyranny, no matter from what source they come—from earth or heaven, from men or gods. Besides, every traveler upon this vast plain should give to every other traveler his best idea as to the road that should be taken. Each is entitled to the honest opinion of all. And there is but one way to get an honest opinion upon any subject whatever. The person giving the opinion must be free from fear. The merchant must not fear to lose his custom, the doctor his practice, nor the preacher his pulpit. There can be no advance without liberty. Suppression of honest inquiry is retrogression, and must end in intellectual night. The tendency of orthodox religion today is toward mental slavery and barbarism. Not one of the orthodox ministers dare preach what he thinks if he knows a majority of his congregation think otherwise. He knows that every member of his church stands guard over his brain with a creed, like a club, in his hand. He knows that he is not expected to search after the truth, but that he is employed to defend the creed. Every pulpit is a pillory, in which stands a hired culprit, defending the justice of his own imprisonment.

Is it desirable that all should be exactly alike in their religious convictions? Is any such thing possible? Do we not know that there are no two persons alike in the whole world? No two trees, no two leaves, no two anythings that are alike? Infinite diversity is the law. Religion tries to force all minds into one mold. Knowing that all cannot believe, the church endeavors to make all say they believe. She longs for the unity of hypocrisy, and detests the splendid diversity of individuality and freedom.

Nearly all people stand in great horror of annihilation, and yet to give up your individuality is to annihilate yourself. Mental slavery is mental death, and every man who has given up his intellectual freedom is the living coffin of his dead soul. In this sense, every church is a cemetery and every creed an epitaph.

We should all remember that to be like other people is to be unlike ourselves, and that nothing can be more detestable in character than servile imitation. The great trouble with imitation is that we are apt to ape those who are in reality far below us. After all, the poorest bargain that a human being can make is to give his individuality for what is called respectability.

There is no saying more degrading than this: "It is better to be the tail of a lion than the head of a dog." It is a responsibility to think and act for yourself. Most people hate responsibility; therefore they join something and become the tail of some lion. They say, "My party can act for me—my church can do my thinking. It is enough for me to pay taxes and obey the lion to which I belong, without troubling myself about the right, the wrong, or the why, or the wherefore of anything whatever." These people are respectable. They hate reformers, and dislike exceedingly to have their minds disturbed. They regard convictions as very disagreeable things to have. They love forms, and enjoy, beyond everything else, telling what a splendid tail their lion has, and what a troublesome dog their neighbor is. Besides, this natural inclination to avoid personal responsibility is, and always has been, the fact that every religionist has warned men against the presumption and wickedness of thinking for themselves. The reason has been denounced by all Christendom as the only unsafe guide. The church has left nothing undone to prevent man following the logic of his brain. The plainest facts have been covered with the mantle of mystery. The grossest absurdities have been declared to be self-evident facts. The order of nature has been, as it were, reversed, that the hypocritical few might govern the honest many. The man who stood by the conclusion of his reason was denounced as a scorner and hater of God and his holy church. From the organization of the first church until this moment, to think your own thoughts has been inconsistent with membership. Every member has borne the marks of collar, and chain, and whip. No man ever seriously attempted to reform a church without being cast out and hunted down by the hounds of hypocrisy. The highest crime against a creed is to change it. Reformation is treason.

Thousands of young men are being educated at this moment by the various churches. What for? In order that they may be prepared to investigate the phenomena by which we are surrounded? No! The object, and the only object, is that they may be prepared to defend a creed; that they may learn the arguments of their respective churches, and repeat them in the dull ears of a thoughtless congregation. If one, after being thus trained at the expense of the Methodists, turns Presbyterian or Baptist, he is denounced as an ungrateful wretch. Honest investigation is utterly impossible within the pale of any church, for the reason, that if you think the church is right you will not investigate, and if you think it wrong, the church will investigate you. The consequence of this is that most of the theological literature is the result of suppression, of fear, tyranny, and hypocrisy.

Every orthodox writer necessarily said to himself, "If I write that, my wife and children may want for bread. I will be covered with shame and branded with infamy; but if I write this, I will gain position, power, and honor. My church rewards defenders, and burns reformers.

Under these conditions all your Scotts, Henrys, and McKnights have written; and weighed in these scales, what are their commentaries worth? They are not the ideas and decisions of honest judges, but the sophisms of the paid attorneys of superstition. Who can tell what the world has lost by this infamous system of suppression? How many grand thinkers have died with the mailed hand of superstition upon their lips? How many splendid ideas have perished in the cradle of the brain, strangled in the poison coils of that python, the Church!

For thousands of years a thinker was hunted down like an escaped convict. To him who had braved the church, every door was shut, every knife was open. To shelter him from the wild storm, to give him a crust when dying, to put a cup of water to his cracked and bleeding lips; these were all crimes, not one of which the church ever did forgive; and with the justice taught of her God, his helpless children were exterminated as scorpions and vipers.

Who at the present day can imagine the courage, the devotion to principle, the intellectual and moral grandeur it once required to be an infidel, to brave the church, her racks, her fagots, her dungeons, her tongues of fire,—to defy and scorn her heaven and her hell—her devil and her God? They were the noblest sons of earth. They were the real saviors of our race, the destroyers of superstition and the creators of Science. They were the real Titans who bared their grand foreheads to all the thunderbolts of the gods.

The church has been, and still is, the great robber. She has rifled not only the pockets but the brains of the world. She is the stone at the sepulcher of liberty; the upas tree, in whose shade the intellect of man has withered; the Gorgon beneath whose gaze the human heart has turned to stone. Under her influence even the Protestant mother expects to be happy in heaven, while her brave boy, who fell fighting for the rights of man, shall writhe in hell.

It is said that some of the Indian tribes place the heads of their children between pieces of bark until the form of the skull is permanently changed. To us this seems a most shocking custom; and yet, after all, is it as bad as to put the souls of our children in the straitjacket of a creed? to so utterly deform their minds that they regard the God of the Bible as a being of infinite mercy, and really consider it a virtue to believe a thing just because it seems unreasonable? Every child in the Christian world has uttered its wondering protest against this outrage. All the machinery of the church is constantly employed in corrupting the reason of children. In every possible way they are robbed of their own thoughts and forced to accept the statements of others. Every Sunday school has for its object the crushing out of every germ of individuality. The poor children are taught that nothing can be more acceptable to God than unreasoning obedience and eyeless faith, and that to believe God did an impossible act is far better than to do a good one yourself. They are told that all religions have been simply the John the Baptists of ours; that all the gods of antiquity have withered and shrunken into the Jehovah of the Jews; that all the longings and aspirations of the race are realized in the motto of the Evangelical Alliance, "Liberty in nonessentials"; that all there is, or ever was, of religion can be found in the apostles' creed; that there is nothing left to be discovered; that all the thinkers are dead, and all the living should simply be believers; that we have only to repeat the epitaph found on the grave of wisdom; that graveyards are the best possible universities, and that the children must be forever beaten with the bones of the fathers.

It has always seemed absurd to suppose that a god would choose for his companions, during all eternity, the dear souls whose highest and only ambition is to obey. He certainly would now and then be tempted to make the same remark made by an English gentleman to his poor guest. The gentleman had invited a man in humble circumstances to dine with him. The man was so overcome with the honor that to everything the gentleman said he replied "Yes." Tired at last with the monotony of acquiescence, the gentleman cried out, "For God's sake, my good man, say 'No' just once, so there will be two of us."

Is it possible that an infinite God created this world simply to be the dwelling place of slaves and serfs? simply for the purpose of raising orthodox Christians? That he did a few miracles to astonish them; that all the evils of life are simply his punishments, and that he is finally going to turn heaven into a kind of religious museum filled with Baptist barnacles, petrified Presbyterians, and Methodist mummies? I want no heaven for which I must give my reason, no happiness in exchange for my liberty, and no immortality that demands the surrender of my individuality. Better rot in the windowless tomb, to which there is no door but the red mouth of the pallid worm, than wear the jeweled collar even of a god.

Religion does not, and cannot, contemplate man as free. She accepts only the homage of the prostrate, and scorns the offerings of those who stand erect. The wide and sunny fields belong not to her domain. The star-lit heights of genius and individuality are above and beyond her appreciation and power. Her subjects cringe at her feet, covered with the dust of obedience. They are not athletes standing posed by rich life and brave endeavor like antique statues, but shriveled deformities, studying with furtive glance the cruel face of power.

No religionist seems capable of comprehending this plain truth. There is this difference between thought and action: for our actions we are responsible to ourselves and to those injuriously affected;

for thoughts, there can, in the nature of things, be no responsibility to gods or men, here or hereafter. And yet the Protestant has vied with the Catholic in denouncing freedom of thought; and while I was taught to hate Catholicism with every drop of my blood, it is only justice to say that in all essential particulars it is precisely the same as every other religion. Luther denounced mental liberty with all the coarse and brutal vigor of his nature; Calvin despised, from the very bottom of his petrified heart, anything that even looked like religious toleration, and solemnly declared that to advocate it was to crucify Christ afresh. All the founders of all the orthodox churches have advocated the same infamous tenet. The truth is, that what is called religion is necessarily inconsistent with free thought.

A believer is a bird in a cage, a Freethinker is an eagle parting the clouds with tireless wing.

At present, owing to the inroads that have been made by liberals and infidels, most of the churches pretend to be in favor of religious liberty. Of these churches, we will ask this question: How can a man, who conscientiously believes in religious liberty, worship a God who does not? They say to us: "We will not imprison you on account of your belief, but our God will." "We will not burn you because you throw away the sacred Scriptures, but their author will." "We think it an infamous crime to persecute our brethren for opinion's sake,—but the God, whom we ignorantly worship, will on that account, damn his own children forever."

Why is it that these Christians not only detest the infidels, but cordially despise each other? Why do they refuse to worship in the temples of each other? Why do they care so little for the damnation of men, and so much for the baptism of children? Why will they adorn their churches with the money of thieves and flatter vice for the sake of subscriptions? Why will they attempt to bribe Science to certify to the writings of God? Why do they torture the words of the great into an acknowledgment of the truth of Christianity? Why do they stand with hat in hand before presidents, kings, emperors, and scientists, begging, like Lazarus, for a few crumbs of religious comfort? Why are they so delighted to find an allusion to providence in the message of Lincoln? Why are they so afraid that some one will find out that Paley wrote an essay in favor of the Epicurean philosophy, and that Sir Isaac Newton was once an infidel? Why are they so anxious to show that Voltaire recanted; that Paine died palsied with fear; that the Emperor Julian cried out "Galilean, thou hast conquered"; that Gibbon died a Catholic; that Agassiz had a little confidence in Moses; that the old Napoleon was once complimentary enough to say that he thought Christ greater than himself or Caesar; that Washington was caught on his knees at Valley Forge; that blunt old Ethan Allen told his child to believe the religion of her mother; that Franklin said, "Don't unchain the tiger"; and that Voleny got frightened in a storm at sea?

Is it because the foundation of their temple is crumbling, because the walls are cracked, the pillars leaning, the great dome swaying to its fall, and because Science has written over the high altar its MENE, MENE, TEKEL, UPHARSIN—the old words, destined to be the epitaph of all religions?

Every assertion of individual independence has been a step toward infidelity. Luther started toward Humboldt,—Wesley, toward John Stuart Mill. To really reform the church is to destroy it. Every new religion has a little less superstition than the old, so that the religion of Science is but a question of time.

I will not say the church has been an unmitigated evil in all respects. Its history is infamous and glorious. It has delighted in the production of extremes. It has furnished murderers for its own martyrs. It has sometimes fed the body, but has always starved the soul. It has been a charitable highwayman—a profligate beggar—a generous pirate. It has produced some angels and a multitude of devils. It has built more prisons than asylums. It made a hundred orphans while it cared for one. In one hand it has carried the alms dish and in the other a sword. It has founded schools and endowed universities for the purpose of destroying true learning. It filled the world with hypocrites and zealots, and upon the cross of its own Christ it crucified the individuality of man. It has sought to destroy the independence of the soul and put the world upon its knees. This is its crime. The commission of this crime was necessary to its existence. In order to compel obedience it declared that it had the truth, and all the truth; that God had made it the keeper of his secrets; his agent and his vicegerent. It declared that all other religions were false and infamous. It rendered all compromise impossible and all thought superfluous. Thought was its enemy, obedience was its friend. Investigation was fraught with danger; therefore investigation was suppressed. The holy of holies was behind the curtain. All this was upon the principle that forgers hate to have the signature examined by an expert, and that imposture detests curiosity.

"He that hath ears to hear, let him hear," has always been the favorite text of the church.

In short, Christianity has always opposed every forward movement of the human race. Across the highway of progress it has always been building breastworks of Bibles, tracts, commentaries, prayer books, creeds, dogmas, and platforms, and at every advance the Christians have gathered together behind these heaps of rubbish and shot the poisoned arrows of malice at the soldiers of freedom.

And even the liberal Christian of today has his holy of holies, and in the niche of the temple of his heart has his idol. He still clings to a part of the old superstition, and all the pleasant memories of the old belief linger in the horizon of his thoughts like a sunset. We associate the memory of those we love with the religion of our childhood. It seems almost a sacrilege to rudely destroy the idols that our fathers worshiped, and turn their sacred and beautiful truths into the fables of barbarism. Some throw away the Old Testament and cling to the New, while others give up everything except the idea that there is a personal God, and that in some wonderful way we are the objects of his care.

Even this, in my opinion, as Science, the great iconoclast, marches onward, will have to be abandoned with the rest. The great ghost will surely share the fate of the little ones. They fled at the first appearance of the dawn, and the other will vanish with the perfect day. Until then the independence of man is little more than a dream. Overshadowed by an immense personality, in the presence of the irresponsible and the infinite, the individuality of man is lost, and he falls prostrate in the very dust of fear. Beneath the frown of the absolute, man stands a wretched, trembling slave,—beneath his smile he is at best only a fortunate serf. Governed by a being whose arbitrary will is law, chained to the chariot of power, his destiny rests in the pleasure of the unknown. Under these circumstances, what wretched object can he have in lengthening out his aimless life?

And yet, in most minds, there is a vague fear of the gods— a shrinking from the malice of the skies. Our fathers were slaves, and nearly all their children are mental serfs. The enfranchisement of the soul is a slow and painful process. Superstition, the mother of those hideous twins, Fear and Faith, from her throne of skulls, still rules the world, and will until the mind of woman ceases to be the property of priests.

When women reason, and babes sit in the lap of philosophy, the victory of reason over the shadowy host of darkness will be complete.

In the minds of many, long after the intellect has thrown aside as utterly fabulous the legends of the church, there still remains a lingering suspicion, born of the mental habits contracted in childhood, that after all there may be a grain of truth in these mountains of theological mist, and that possibly the superstitious side is the side of safety.

A gentleman, walking among the ruins of Athens, came upon a fallen statue of Jupiter; making an exceedingly low bow he said: "O Jupiter! I salute thee." He then added: "Should you ever sit upon the throne of heaven again, do not, I pray you, forget that I treated you politely when you were prostrate."

We have all been taught by the church that nothing is so well calculated to excite the ire of the Deity as to express a doubt as to his existence, and that to deny it is an unpardonable sin.

Numerous well-attested instances are referred to of atheists being struck dead for denying the existence of God. According to these religious people, God is infinitely above us in every respect, infinitely merciful, and yet he cannot bear to hear a poor finite man honestly question his existence. Knowing, as he does, that his children are groping in darkness and struggling with doubt and fear; knowing that he could enlighten them if he would, he still holds the expression of a sincere doubt as to his existence, the most infamous of crimes. According to orthodox logic, God having furnished us with imperfect minds, has a right to demand a perfect result.

Suppose Mr. Smith should overhear a couple of small bugs holding a discussion as to the existence of Mr. Smith, and suppose one should have the temerity to declare, upon the honor of a bug, that he had examined the whole question to the best of his ability, including the argument based upon design, and had come to the conclusion that no man by the name of Smith had ever lived. Think then of Mr. Smith flying into an ecstasy of rage, crushing the atheist bug beneath his iron heel, while he exclaimed, "I will teach you, blasphemous wretch, that Smith is a diabolical fact!" What then can we think of a God who would open the artillery of heaven upon one of his own children for simply expressing his honest thought? And what man who really thinks can help repeating the words of Ennius: "If there are gods they certainly pay no attention to the affairs of man."

Think of the millions of men and women who have been destroyed simply for loving and worshiping this God. Is it possible that this God, having infinite power, saw his loving and heroic children languishing in the darkness of dungeons; heard the clank of their chains when they lifted their hands to him in the agony of prayer; saw them stretched upon the bigot's rack, where death alone had pity; saw the serpents of flame crawl hissing round their shrinking forms—saw all this for sixteen hundred years, and sat as silent as a stone?

From such a God, why should man expect assistance? Why should he waste his days in fruitless prayer? Why should he fall upon his knees and implore a phantom—a phantom that is deaf, and dumb, and blind?

Although we live in what is called a free government,—and politically we are free,—there is but little religious liberty in America. Society demands either that you belong to some church, or that you suppress your opinions. It is contended by many that ours is a Christian government, founded upon the Bible, and that all who look upon that book as false or foolish are destroying the foundation of our country. The truth is, our government is not founded upon the rights of gods, but upon the rights of men. Our Constitution was framed, not to declare and uphold the deity of Christ, but the sacredness of humanity. Ours is the first government made by the people and for the people. It is the only nation with which the gods have had nothing to do. And yet there are some judges dishonest and cowardly enough to solemnly decide that this is a Christian country, and that our free institutions are based upon the infamous laws of Jehovah. Such judges are the Jeffries of the church. They believe that decisions, made by hirelings at the bidding of kings, are binding upon man forever. They regard old law as far superior to modern justice. They are what might be called orthodox judges. They spend their days in finding out not what ought to be, but what has been. With their backs to the sunrise they worship the night. There is only one future event with which they concern themselves, and that is their re-election. No honest court ever did, or ever will, decide that our Constitution is Christian. The Bible teaches that the powers that be are ordained of God. The Bible teaches that God is the source of all authority, and that all kings have obtained their power from him. Every tyrant has claimed to be the agent of the Most High. The Inquisition was founded not in the name of man, but in the name of God. All the governments of Europe recognize the greatness of God, and the littleness of the people. In all ages, hypocrites, called priests, have put crowns upon the heads of thieves, called kings.

The Declaration of Independence announces the sublime truth, that all power comes from the people. This was a denial, and the first denial of a nation, of the infamous dogma that God confers the right upon one man to govern others. It was the first grand assertion of the dignity of the human race. It declared the governed to be the source of power, and in fact denied the authority of any and all gods. Through the ages of slavery—through the weary centuries of the lash and chain, God was the acknowledged ruler of the world. To enthrone man was to dethrone Him.

To Paine, Jefferson, and Franklin are we indebted, more than to all others, for a human government, and for a Constitution in which no God is recognized superior to the legally expressed will of the people.

They knew that to put God in the Constitution was to put man out. They knew that the recognition of a Deity would be seized upon by fanatics and zealots as a pretext for destroying the liberty of thought. They knew the terrible history of the church too well to place in her keeping, or in the keeping of her God, the sacred rights of man. They intended that all should have the right to worship, or not to worship; that our laws should make no distinction on account of creed. They intended to found and frame a government for man, and for man alone. They wished to preserve the individuality and liberty of all; to prevent the few from governing the many, and the many from persecuting and destroying the few.

Notwithstanding all this, the spirit of persecution still lingers in our laws. In many of the States, only those who believe in the existence of some kind of God are under the protection of the law.

The supreme court of Illinois decided, in the year of grace 1856, that an unbeliever in the existence of an intelligent First Cause could not be allowed to testify in any court. His wife and children might have been murdered before his very face, and yet in the absence of other witnesses, the murderer could not have even been indicted. The atheist was a legal outcast. To him, Justice was not only blind, but deaf. He was liable, like other men, to support the Government, and was forced to contribute his share towards paying the salaries of the very judges who decided that under no circumstances could his voice be heard in any court. This was the law of Illinois, and so remained until the adoption of the new Constitution. By such infamous means has the church endeavored to chain the human mind, and protect the majesty of her God. The fact is, we have no national religion, and no national God; but every citizen is allowed to have a religion and a God of his own, or to reject all religions and deny the existence of all gods. The church, however, never has, and never will understand and appreciate the genius of our Government.

Last year, in a convention of Protestant bigots, held in the city of New York for the purpose of creating public opinion in favor of a religious amendment to the Federal Constitution, a reverend doctor of divinity, speaking of atheists, said: "What are the rights of the atheist? I would tolerate him as I would tolerate a poor lunatic. I would tolerate him as I would tolerate a con-spirator. He may live and go free, hold his lands and enjoy his home—he may even vote; but for any higher or more advanced citizenship, he is, as I hold, utterly disqualified." These are the sentiments of the church today.

Give the church a place in the Constitution, let her touch once more the sword of power, and the priceless fruit of all the ages will turn to ashes on the lips of men.

In religious ideas and conceptions there has been for ages a slow and steady development. At the bottom of the ladder (speaking of modern times) is Catholicism, and at the top is Science. The intermediate rounds of this ladder are occupied by the various sects, whose name is legion.

But whatever may be the truth upon any subject has nothing to do with our right to investigate that subject, and express any opinion we may form. All that I ask is the same right I freely accord to all others.

A few years ago a Methodist clergyman took it upon himself to give me a piece of friendly advice. "Although you may disbelieve the Bible," said he, "you ought not to say so. That, you should keep to yourself."

"Do you believe the Bible," said I.

He replied, "Most assuredly."

To which I retorted, "Your answer conveys no information to me. You may be following your own advice. You told me to suppress my opinions. Of course a man who will advise others to dissimulate will not always be particular about telling the truth himself."

There can be nothing more utterly subversive of all that is really valuable than the suppression of honest thought. No man, worthy of the form he bears, will at the command of church or state solemnly repeat a creed his reason scorns.

It is the duty of each and every one to maintain his individuality. "This above all, to thine own self be true, and it must follow as the night the day, thou canst not then be false to any man." It is a magnificent thing to be the sole proprietor of yourself. It is a terrible thing to wake up at night and say, "There is nobody in this bed." It is humiliating to know that your ideas are all borrowed; that you are indebted to your memory for your principles; that your religion is simply one of your habits, and that you would have convictions only if they were contagious. It is mortifying to feel that you belong to a mental mob and cry "crucify him," because others do; that you reap what the great and brave have sown; and that you can benefit the world only by leaving it.

Surely every human being ought to attain the dignity of the *unit.* Surely it is worth something to be *one,* and to feel that the census of the universe would be incomplete without counting you. Surely there is grandeur in knowing that in the realm of thought, at least, you are without a chain; that you have the right to explore all heights and all depths; that there are no walls nor fences, nor prohibited places, nor sacred corners in all the vast expanse of thought; that your intellect owes no allegiance to any being, human or divine; that you hold all in fee and upon no condition and by no tenure whatever; that in the world of mind you are relieved from all personal dictation, and from the ignorant tyranny of majorities. Surely it is worth something to feel that there are no priests, no popes, no parties, no governments, no kings, no gods, to whom your intellect can be forced to pay a reluctant homage. Surely it is a joy to know that all the cruel ingenuity of bigotry can devise no prison, no dungeon, no cell in which for one instant to confine a thought; that ideas cannot be dislocated by racks, nor crushed in iron boots, nor burned with fire. Surely it is sublime to think that the brain is a castle, and that within its curious bastions and winding halls the soul, in spite of all worlds and all beings, is the supreme sovereign of itself.

HERETICS AND HERESIES

HERETICS AND HERESIES

LIBERTY, A WORD WITHOUT WHICH
ALL OTHER WORDS ARE VAIN

Whoever has an opinion of his own, and honestly expresses it, will be guilty of heresy. Heresy is what the minority believe; it is the name given by the powerful to the doctrine of the weak. This word was born of the hatred, arrogance, and cruelty of those who love their enemies, and who, when smitten on one cheek, turn the other. This word was born of intellectual slavery in the feudal ages of thought. It was an epithet used in the place of argument. From the commencement of the Christian era, every art has been exhausted and every conceivable punishment inflicted to force all people to hold the same religious opinions. This effort was born of the idea that a certain belief was necessary to the salvation of the soul. Christ taught, and the church still teaches, that unbelief is the blackest of crimes. God is supposed to hate, with an infinite and implacable hatred, every heretic upon the earth, and the heretics who have died are supposed at this moment to be suffering the agonies of the damned. The church persecutes the living and her God burns the dead.

It is claimed that God wrote a book called the Bible, and

it is generally admitted that this book is somewhat difficult to understand. As long as the church had all the copies of this book, and the people were not allowed to read it, there was comparatively little heresy in the world; but when it was printed and read, people began honestly to differ as to its meaning. A few were independent and brave enought to give the world their real thoughts, and for the extermination of these men the church used all her power. Protestants and Catholics vied with each other in the work of enslaving the human mind. For ages they were rivals in the infamous effort to rid the earth of honest people. They infested every country, every city, town, hamlet, and family. They appealed to the worst passions of the human heart. They sowed the seeds of discord and hatred in every land. Brother denounced brother; wives informed against their husbands; mothers accused their children; dungeons were crowded with the innocent; the flesh of the good and true rotted in the clasp of chains; the flames devoured the heroic; and in the name of the most merciful God, his children were exterminated with famine, sword, and fire. Over the wild waves of battle rose and fell the banner of Jesus Christ. For sixteen hundred years the robes of the church were red with innocent blood. The ingenuity of Christians was exhausted in devising punishment severe enough to be inflicted upon other Christians who honestly and sincerely differed with them upon any point whatever.

Give any orthodox church the power, and today they would punish heresy with whip, and chain, and fire. As long as a church deems a certain belief essential to salvation, just so long it will kill and burn if it has the power. Why should the church pity a man whom her God hates? Why should she show mercy to a kind and noble heretic whom her God will burn in eternal fire? Why should a Christian be better than his God? It is impossible for the imagination to conceive of a greater atrocity than has been perpetrated by the church. Every nerve in the human body capable of pain has been sought out and touched by the church.

Let it be remembered that all churches have persecuted heretics to the extent of their power. Toleration has increased only when and where the power of the church has diminished. From Augustine until now the spirit of the Christians has remained the same. There has been the same intolerance, the same undying hatred of all who think for themselves, and the same determination to crush out of the human brain all knowledge inconsistent with an ignorant creed.

Every church pretends that it has a revelation from God, and that this revelation must be given to the people through the church; that the church acts through its priests; and that ordinary mortals must be content with a revelation—not from God—but from the church. Had the people submitted to this preposterous claim, of course there could have been but one church, and that church never could have advanced. It might have retrograded, because it is not necessary to think or investigate in order to forget. Without heresy there could have been no progress.

The highest type of the orthodox Christian does not forget; neither does he learn. He neither advances nor recedes. He is a living fossil embedded in that rock called faith. He makes no effort to better his condition, because all his strength is exhausted in keeping other people from improving theirs. The supreme desire of his heart is to force all others to adopt his creed, and in order to accomplish this object he denounces free thinking as a crime, and this crime he calls heresy. When he had power, heresy was the most terrible and formidable of words. It meant confiscation, exile, imprisonment, torture, and death.

In those days the cross and rack were inseparable companions. Across the open Bible lay the sword and fagot. Not content with burning such heretics as were alive, they even tried the dead, in order that the church might rob their wives and children. The property of all heretics was confiscated, and on this account they charged the dead with being heretical—indicted, as it were, their dust—to the end that the church might clutch the bread of orphans. Learned divines discussed the propriety of tearing out the tongues of heretics before they were burned, and the general opinion was that this ought to be done so that the heretics should not be able, by uttering blasphemies, to shock the Christians who were burning them. With a mixture of ferocity and Christianity, the priests insisted that heretics ought to be burned at a slow fire, giving as a reason that more time was given them for repentance.

No wonder that Jesus Christ said, "I came not to bring peace, but a sword."

Every priest regarded himself as the agent of God. He answered all questions by authority, and to treat him with disrespect was an insult offered to God. No one was asked to think, but all were commanded to obey.

In 1208 the Inquisition was established. Seven years afterward, the fourth council of the Lateran enjoined all kings and rulers to swear an oath that they would exterminate heretics from their dominions. The sword of the church was unsheathed, and the world was at the mercy of ignorant and infuriated priests, whose eyes feasted upon the agonies they inflicted. Acting, as they believed, or pretended to believe, under the command of God; stimulated by the hope of infinite reward in another world—hating heretics with every drop of their bestial blood; savage beyond description; merciless beyond conception,—these infamous priests, in a kind of frenzied joy, leaped upon the helpless victims of their rage. They crushed their bones in iron boots; tore their quivering flesh with iron hooks and pincers; cut off their lips and eyelids; pulled out their nails, and into the bleeding quick thrust needles; tore out their tongues; extinguished their eyes; stretched them upon racks; flayed them alive; crucified them with their heads downward; exposed them to wild beasts; burned them at the stake; mocked their cries and groans; ravished their wives; robbed their children; and then prayed to God to finish the holy work in hell.

Millions upon millions were sacrificed upon the altars of bigotry. The Catholic burned the Lutheran, the Lutheran burned the Catholic, the Episcopalian tortured the Presbyterian, the Presbyterian tortured the Episcopalian. Every denomination killed all it could of every other; and each Christian felt duty bound to exterminate every other Christian who denied the smallest fraction of his creed.

In the reign of Henry VIII—that pious and moral founder of the apostolic Episcopal Church,—there was passed by the parliament of England an act entitled "An act for abolishing of diversity of opinion." And in this act was set forth what a good Christian was obliged to believe:

First, That in the sacrament was the real body and blood of Jesus Christ.

Second, That the body and blood of Jesus Christ was in the bread, and the blood and body of Jesus Christ was in the wine.

Third, That priests should not marry.

Fourth, That vows of chastity were of perpetual obligation.

Fifth, That private masses ought to be continued; and,

Sixth, That auricular confession to a priest must be maintained.

This creed was made by law, in order that all men might know just what to believe by simply reading the statute. The church hated to see the people wearing out their brains in thinking upon these subjects. It was thought far better that a creed should be made by parliament, so that whatever might be lacking in evidence might be made up in force. The punishment for denying the first article was death by fire. For the denial of any other article, imprisonment, and for the second offense—death.

Your attention is called to these six articles, established during the reign of Henry VIII, and by the Church of England, simply because not one of these articles is believed by that church today. If the law then made by the church could be enforced now, every Episcopalian would be burned at the stake.

Similar laws were passed in most Christian countries, as all orthodox churches firmly believed that mankind could be legislated into heaven. According to the creed of every church, slavery leads to heaven, liberty leads to hell. It was claimed that God had founded the church, and that to deny the authority of the church was to be a traitor to God, and consequently an ally of the devil. To torture and destroy one of the soldiers of Satan was a duty no good Christian cared to neglect. Nothing can be sweeter than to earn the gratitude of God by killing your own enemies. Such a mingling of profit and revenge, of heaven for yourself and damnation for those you dislike, is a temptation that your ordinary Christian never resists.

According to the theologians, God, the Father of us all, wrote a letter to his children. The children have always differed somewhat as to the meaning of this letter. In consequence of these honest differences, these brothers began to cut out each other's hearts. In every land, where this letter from God has been read, the children to whom and for whom it was written have been filled with hatred and malice. They have imprisoned and murdered each other, and the wives and children of each other. In the name of God every possible crime has been committed, every conceivable outrage has been perpetrated. Brave men, tender and loving women, beautiful girls, and prattling babes have been exterminated in the name of Jesus Christ. For more than fifty generations the church has carried the black flag. Her vengeance has been measured only by her power. During all these years of infamy no heretic has ever been forgiven. With the heart of a fiend she has hated; with the clutch of avarice she has grasped; with the jaws of a dragon she has devoured; pitiless as famine, merciless as fire, with the conscience of a serpent: such is the history of the Church of God.

I do not say, and I do not believe, that Christians are as bad as their creeds. In spite of church and dogma, there have been millions and millions of men and women true to the loftiest and most generous promptings of the human heart. They have been true to their convictions, and, with a self-denial and fortitude excelled by none, have labored and suffered for the salvation of men. Imbued with the spirit of self-sacrifice, believing that by personal effort they could rescue at least a few souls from the infinite shadow of hell, they have cheerfully endured every hardship and scorned every danger. And yet, notwithstanding all this, they believed that honest error was a crime. They knew that the Bible so declared, and they believed that all unbelievers would be eternally lost. They believed that religion was of God, and all heresy of the devil. They killed heretics in defense of their own souls and the souls of their children. They killed them because, according to their idea, they were the enemies of God, and because the Bible teaches that the blood of the unbeliever is a most acceptable sacrifice to heaven.

Nature never prompted a loving mother to throw her child into the Ganges. Nature never prompted men to exterminate each other for a difference of opinion concerning the baptism of infants. These crimes have been produced by religions filled with all that is illogical, cruel, and hideous. These religions were produced for the most part by ignorance, tyranny, and hypocrisy. Under the impression that the infinite ruler and creator of the universe had commanded the destruction of heretics and infidels, the church perpetrated all these crimes.

Men and women have been burned for thinking there is but one God; that there was none; that the Holy Ghost is younger than God; that God was somewhat older than his son; for insisting that good works will save a man without faith; that faith will do without good works; for declaring that a sweet babe will not be burned eternally, because its parents failed to have its head wet by a priest; for speaking of God as though he had a nose; for denying that Christ was his own father; for contending that three persons, rightly added together, make more than one; for believing in purgatory; for denying the reality of hell; for pretending that priests can forgive sins; for preaching that God is an essence; for denying that witches rode through the air on sticks; for doubting the total depravity of the human heart; for laughing at irresistible grace, predestination, and particular redemption; for denying that good bread could be made of the body of a dead man; for pretending that the pope was not managing this world for God, and in the place of God; for disputing the efficacy of a vicarious atonement; for thinking the Virgin Mary was born like other people; for thinking that a man's rib was hardly sufficient to make a good-sized woman; for denying that God used his finger for a pen; for asserting that prayers are not answered, that diseases are not sent to punish unbelief; for denying the authority of the Bible; for having a Bible in their possession; for attending mass, and for refusing to attend; for wearing a surplice; for carrying a cross, and for refusing; for being a Catholic, and for being a Protestant; for being an Episcopalian, a Presbyterian, a Baptist, and for being a Quaker. In short, every virtue has been a crime, and every crime a virtue. The church has burned honesty and rewarded hypocrisy. And all this, because it was commanded by a book—a book that men had been taught implicitly to believe, long before they knew one word that was in it. They had been taught that to doubt the truth of this book—to examine it, even—was a crime of such enormity that it could not be forgiven, either in this world or in the next.

The Bible was the real persecutor. The Bible burned heretics, built dungeons, founded the Inquisition, and trampled upon all the liberties of men.

How long, O how long will mankind worship a book? How long will they grovel in the dust before the ignorant legends of the barbaric past? How long, O how long will they pursue phantoms in a darkness deeper than death?

Unfortunately for the world, about the beginning of the sixteenth century, a man by the name of Gerard Chauvin was married to Jeanne Lefranc, and still more unfortunately for the world, the fruit of this marriage was a son, called John Chauvin, who afterwards became famous as John Calvin, the founder of the Presbyterian Church.

This man forged five fetters for the brain. These fetters he called points. That is to say, predestination, particular redemption, total depravity, irresistible grace, and the perseverance of the saints. About the neck of each follower he put a collar bristling with these five iron points. The presence of all these points on the collar is still the test of orthodoxy in the church he founded. This man, when in the flush of youth, was elected to the office of preacher in Geneva. He at once, in union with Farel, drew up a condensed statement of the Presbyterian doctrine, and all the citizens of Geneva, on pain of banishment, were compelled to take an oath that they believed this statement. Of this proceeding Calvin very innocently remarked that it produced great satisfaction. A man named Caroli had the audacity to dispute with Calvin. For this outrage he was banished.

To show you what great subjects occupied the attention of Calvin, it is only necessary to state that he furiously discussed the question as to whether the sacramental bread should be leavened or unleavened. He drew up laws regulating the cut of the citizens' clothes, and prescribing their diet, and all those whose garments were not in the Calvin fashion were refused the sacrament. At last, the people becoming tired of this petty theological tyranny, banished Calvin. In a few years, however, he was recalled and received with great enthusiasm. After this he was supreme, and the will of Calvin became the law of Geneva.

Under his benign administration, James Gruet was beheaded because he had written some profane verses. The slightest word against Calvin or his absurd doctrines was punished as a crime.

In 1553 a man was tried at Vienne by the Catholic Church for heresy. He was convicted and sentenced to death by burning. It was apparently his good fortune to escape. Pursued by the sleuth hounds of intolerance he fled to Geneva for protection. A dove flying from hawks sought safety in the nest of a vulture. This fugitive from the cruelty of Rome asked shelter from John Calvin, who had writen a book in favor of religious toleration. Servetus had forgotten that this book was written by Calvin when in the minority; that it was written in weakness to be forgotten in power; that it was produced by fear instead of principle. He did not know that Calvin had caused his arrest at Vienne, in France, and had sent a copy of his work, which was claimed to be blasphemous, to the archbishop. He did not then know that the Protestant Calvin was acting as one of the detectives of the Catholic Church, and had been instrumental in procuring his conviction for heresy. Ignorant of all this unspeakable infamy, he put himself in the power of this very Calvin. The maker of the Presbyterian creed caused the fugitive Servetus to be arrested for blasphemy. He was tried. Calvin was his accuser. He was convicted and condemned to death by fire. On the morning of the fatal day, Calvin saw him, and Servetus, the victim, asked forgiveness of Calvin, the murderer. Servetus was bound to the stake, and the fagots were lighted. The wind carried the flames somewhat away from his body, so that he slowly roasted for hours. Vainly he implored a speedy death. At last the flames climbed round his form; through smoke and fire his murderers saw a white heroic face. And there they watched until a man became a charred and shriveled mass.

Liberty was banished from Geneva, and nothing but Presbyterianism was left. Honor, justice, mercy, reason, and charity were all exiled, but the five points of predestination, particular redemption, irresistible grace, total depravity, and the certain perseverance of the saints remained instead.

Calvin founded a little theocracy, modeled after the Old Testament, and succeeded in erecting the most detestable government that ever existed, except the one from which it was copied.

Against all this intolerance, one man, a minister, raised his voice. The name of this man should never be forgotten. It was Castalio. This brave man had the goodness and the courage to declare the innocence of honest error. He was the first of the so-called reformers to take this noble ground. I wish I had the genius to pay a fitting tribute to his memory. Perhaps it would be impossible to pay him a grander compliment than to say, Castalio was in all things the opposite of Calvin. To plead for the right of individual judgment was considered a crime, and Castalio was driven from Geneva by John Calvin. By him he was denounced as a child of the devil, as a dog of Satan, as a beast from hell, and as one who, by this horrid blasphemy of the innocence of honest error, crucified Christ afresh, and by him he was pursued until rescued by the hand of death.

Upon the name of Castalio, Calvin heaped every epithet, until his malice was nearly satisfied and his imagination entirely exhausted. It is impossible to conceive how human nature can become so frightfully perverted as to pursue a fellowman with the malignity of a fiend, simply because he is good, just, and generous.

Calvin was of a pallid, bloodless complexion, thin, sickly, irritable, gloomy, impatient, egotistic, tyrannical, heartless, and infamous. He was a strange compound of revengeful morality, malicious forgiveness, ferocious charity, egotistic humility, and a kind of hellish justice. In other words, he was as near like the God of the Old Testament as his health permitted.

The best thing, however, about the Presbyterians of Geneva was that they denied the power of the Pope, and the best thing about the Pope was that he was not a Presbyterian.

The doctrines of Calvin spread rapidly, and were eagerly accepted by multitudes on the continent; but Scotland, in a few years, became the real fortress of Presbyterianism. The Scotch succeeded in establishing the same kind of theocracy that flourished in Geneva. The clergy took possession and control of everybody and everything. It is impossible to exaggerate the mental degradation, the abject superstition of the people of Scotland during the reign of Presbyterianism. Heretics were hunted and devoured as though they had been wild beasts. The gloomy insanity of Presbyterianism took possession of a great majority of the people. They regarded their ministers as the Jews did Moses and Aaron. They believed that they were the especial agents of God, and that whatsoever they bound in Scotland would be bound in heaven. There was not one particle of intellectual freedom. No man was allowed to differ with the church, or to even contradict a priest. Had Presbyterianism maintained its ascendency, Scotland would have been peopled by savages today.

The revengeful spirit of Calvin took possession of the Puritans, and caused them to redden the soil of the New World with the brave blood of honest men. Clinging to the five points of Calvin, they too established governments in accordance with the teachings of the Old Testament. They too attached the penalty of death to the expression of honest thought. They too believed their church supreme, and exerted all their power to curse this continent with a spiritual despotism as infamous as it was absurd. They believed with Luther that universal toleration is universal error, and universal error is universal hell. Toleration was denounced as a crime.

Fortunately for us, civilization has had a softening effect even upon the Presbyterian Church. To the ennobling influence of the arts and sciences the savage spirit of Calvinism has, in some slight degree, succumbed. True, the old creed remains substantially as it was written, but by a kind of tacit understanding it has come to be regarded as a relic of the past. The cry of "heresy" has been growing fainter and fainter, and, as a consequence, the ministers of that denomination have ventured, now and then, to express doubts as to the damnation of infants, and the doctrine of total depravity. The fact is, the old ideas became a little monotonous to the people. The fall of man, the scheme of redemption and irresistible grace, began to have a familiar sound. The preachers told the old stories while the congregations slept. Some of the ministers became tired of these stories themselves. The five points grew dull, and they felt that nothing short of irresistible grace could bear this endless repetition. The outside world was full of progress, and in every direction men advanced, while this church, anchored to a creed, idly rotted at the shore. Other denominations, imbued some little with the spirit of investigation, were springing up on every side, while the old Presbyterian ark rested on the Ararat of the past, filled with the theological monsters of another age.

Lured by the splendors of the outer world, tempted by the achievements of science, longing to feel the throb and beat of the mighty march of the human race, a few of the ministers of this conservative denomination were compelled, by irresistible sense, to say a few words in harmony with the splendid ideas of today.

These utterances have upon several occasions so nearly wakened some of the members that, rubbing their eyes, they have feebly inquired whether these grand ideas were not somewhat heretical. These ministers found that just in the proportion that their orthodoxy decreased, their congregations increased. Those who dealt in the pure unadulterated article found themselves demonstrating the five points to a less number of hearers than they had points. Stung to madness by this bitter truth, this galling contrast, this harassing fact, the really orthodox have raised the cry of heresy, and expect with this cry to seal the lips of honest men. One of the Presbyterian ministers, and one who has been enjoying the luxury of a little honest thought, and the real rapture of expressing it, has already been indicted, and is about to be tried by the Presbytery of Illinois. He is charged—

First. With having neglected to preach that most comforting and consoling truth, the eternal damnation of the soul.

Surely, that man must be a monster who could wish to blot this blessed doctrine out and rob earth's wretched children of this blissful hope!

Who can estimate the misery that has been caused by this most infamous doctrine of eternal punishment? Think of the lives it has blighted—of the tears it has caused—of the agony it has produced. Think of the millions who have been driven to insanity by this most terrible of dogmas. This doctrine renders God the basest and most cruel being in the universe. Compared with him, the most frightful deities of the most barbarous and degraded tribes are miracles of goodness and mercy. There is nothing more degrading than to worship such a god. Lower than this the soul can never sink. If the doctrine of eternal damnation is true, let me share the fate of the unconverted; let me have my portion in hell, rather than in heaven with a god infamous enough to inflict eternal misery upon any of the sons of men.

Second. With having spoken a few kind words of Robert Collyer and John Stuart Mill.

I have the honor of a slight acquaintance with Robert Collyer. I have read with pleasure some of his exquisite productions. He has a brain full of the dawn, the head of a philosopher, the imagination of a poet, and the sincere heart of a child.

Is a minister to be silenced because he speaks fairly of a noble and candid adversary? Is it a crime to compliment a lover of justice, an advocate of liberty; one who devotes his life to the elevation of man, the discovery of truth, and the promulgation of what he believes to be right?

Can that tongue be palsied by a prebytery that praises a self-denying and heroic life? Is it a sin to speak a charitable word over the grave of John Stuart Mill? Is it heretical to pay a just and graceful tribute to departed worth? Must the true Presbyterian violate the sanctity of the tomb, dig open the grave, and ask his God to curse the silent dust? Is Presbyterianism so narrow that it conceives of no excellence, of no purity of intention, of no spiritual and moral grandeur outside of its barbaric creed? Does it still retain within its stony heart all the malice of its founder? Is it still warming its fleshless hands at the flames that consumed Servetus? Does it still glory in the damnation of infants, and does it still persist in emptying the cradle in order that perdition may be filled? Is it still starving the soul and famishing the heart? Is it still trembling and shivering, crouching, and crawling before its ignorant Confession of Faith?

Had men such as Robert Collyer and John Stuart Mill been present at the burning of Servetus, they would have extinguished the flames with their tears. Had the presbytery of Chicago been there, they would have quietly turned their backs, solemnly divided their coat tails, and warmed themselves.

Third. With having spoken disparagingly of the doctrine of predestination.

If there is any dogma that ought to be protected by law, predestination is that doctrine. Surely it is a cheerful, joyous thing, to one who is laboring, struggling, and suffering in this weary world, to think that before he existed; before the earth was; before a star had glittered in the heavens; before a ray of light had left the quiver of the sun, his destiny had been irrevocably fixed, and that for an eternity before his birth he had been doomed to bear eternal pain.

Fourth. With failing to preach the efficacy of a "vicarious sacrifice."

Suppose a man had been convicted of murder, and was about to be hanged—the governor acting as the executioner; and suppose that just as the doomed man was about to suffer death some one in the crowd should step forward and say, "I am willing to die in the place of that murderer. He has a family, and I have none." And suppose further that the governor should reply, "Come forward, young man, your offer is accepted. A murder has been committed and somebody must be hung, and your death will satisfy the law just as well as the death of the murderer." What would you then think of the doctrine of "vicarious sacrifice"?

This doctrine is the consummation of two outrages—forgiving one crime and committing another.

Fifth. With having inculcated a phase of the doctrine commonly known as "evolution," or "development."

The church believes and teaches the exact opposite of this doctrine. According to the philosophy of theology, man has continued to degenerate for six thousand years. To teach that there is that in nature which impels to higher forms and grander ends, is heresy, of course. The Deity will damn Spencer and his "Evolution," Darwin and his "Origin of Species," Bastian and his "Spontaneous Generation," Huxley and his "Protoplasm," Tyndall and his "Prayer Gauge," and will save those, and those only, who declare that the universe has been cursed, from the smallest atom to the grandest star; that everything tends to evil and to that only; and that the only perfect thing in nature is the Presbyterian Confession of Faith.

Sixth. With having intimated that the reception of Socrates and Penelope at heaven's gate was, to say the least, a trifle more cordial than that of Catherine II.

Penelope, waiting patiently and trustfully for her lord's return, delaying her suitors, while sadly weaving and unweaving the shroud of Laertes, is the most perfect type of wife and woman produced by the civilization of Greece.

Socrates, whose life was above reproach and whose death was beyong all praise, stands today, in the estimation of every thoughtful man, at least the peer of Christ.

Catherine II assassinated her husband. Stepping upon his corpse, she mounted the throne. She was the murderess of Prince Iwan, grand nephew of Peter the Great, who was imprisoned for eighteen years, and who during all that time saw the sky but once. Taken all in all, Catherine was probably one of the most intellectual beasts that ever wore a crown.

Catherine, however, was the head of the Greek Church, Socrates was a heretic and Penelope lived and died without having once heard of "particular redemption" or of "irresistible grace."

Seventh. With repudiating the idea of a "call" to the ministry, and pretending that men were "called" to preach as they were to the other avocations of life.

If this doctrine is true, God, to say the least of it, is an exceedingy poor judge of human nature. It is more than a century since a man of true genius has been found in an orthodox pulpit. Every minister is heretical just to the extent that his intellect is above the average. The Lord seems to be satisfied with mediocrity; but the people are not.

An old deacon, wishing to get rid of an unpopular preacher, advised him to give up the ministry and turn his attention to something else. The preacher replied that he could not conscientiously desert the pulpit, as he had had a "call" to the ministry. To which the deacon replied, "That may be so, but it's very unfortunate for you that when God called you to preach, he forgot to call anybody to hear you."

There is nothing more stupidly egotistic than the claim of the clergy that they are in some divine sense set apart to the service of the Lord; that they have been chosen, and sanctified; that there is an infinite difference between them and persons employed in secular affairs. They teach us that all other professions must take care of themselves; that God allows anybody to be a doctor, a lawyer, statesman, soldier, or artist; that the Motts and Coopers— the Mansfields and Marshalls—the Wilberforces and Sumners— the Angelos and Raphaels, were never honored by a "call." They chose their professions and won their laurels without the assistance of the Lord. All these men were left free to follow their own inclinations, while God was busily engaged selecting and "calling" priests, rectors, elders, ministers, and exhorters.

Eighth. With having doubted that God was the author of the 109th Psalm.

The portion of that psalm which carries with it the clearest and most satisfactory evidences of inspiration, and which has afforded almost unspeakable consolation to the Presbyterian Church, is as follows:

Set thou a wicked man over him; and let Satan stand at his right hand.

When he shall be judged, let him be condemned; and let his prayer become sin.

Let his days be few; and let another take his office.

Let his children be fatherless and his wife a widow.

Let his children be continually vagabonds, and beg; let them seek their bread also out of their desolate places.

Let the extortioner catch all that he hath; and let the stranger spoil his labor.

Let there be none to extend mercy unto him; neither let there be any to favor his fatherless children.

Let his posterity be cut off; and in the generation following let their name be blotted out.

*   *   *   *   *   *   *   *   *   *   *   *

But do thou for me, O God the Lord, for Thy name's sake; because Thy mercy is good, deliver Thou me. * * I will greatly praise the Lord with my *mouth.*

Think of a God wicked and malicious enough to inspire this prayer. Think of one infamous enough to answer it.

Had this inspired psalm been found in some temple erected for the worship of snakes, or in the possession of some cannibal king, written with blood upon the dried skins of babes, there would have been a perfect harmony between its surroundings and its sentiments.

No wonder that the author of this inspired psalm coldly received Socrates and Penelope, and reserved his sweetest smiles for Catherine the Second.

Ninth. With having said that the battles in which the Israelites engaged, with the approval and command of Jehovah, surpassed in cruelty those of Julius Caesar.

Was it Julius Caesar who said, "And the Lord our God delivered him before us; and we smote him, and his sons, and all his people. And we took all his cities, and utterly destroyed the men, and the women, and the little ones, of every city, we left none to remain"?

Did Julius Caesar send the following report to the Roman senate? "And we took all his cities at that time, there was not a city which we took not from them, three score cities, all the region of Argob, the kingdom of Og in Bashan. All these cities were fenced with high walls, gates, and bars; beside unwalled towns a great many. And we utterly destroyed them, as we did unto Sihon, king of Heshbon, utterly destroying the men, women, and children of every city."

Did Caesar take the city of Jericho "and utterly destroy all that was in the city, both men and women, young and old"? Did he smite "all the country of the hills, and of the south, and of the vale, and of the springs, and all their kings, and leave none remaining that breathed, as the Lord God had commanded"?

Search the records of the whole world, find out the history of every barbarous tribe, and you can find no crime that touched a lower depth of infamy than those the Bible's God commanded and approved. For such a God I have no words to express my loathing and contempt, and all the words in all the languages of man would scarcely be sufficient. Away with such a God! Give me Jupiter rather, with Io and Europa, or even Siva with his skulls and snakes.

Tenth. With having repudiated the doctrine of "total depravity."

What a precious doctrine is that of the total depravity of the human heart! How sweet it is to believe that the lives of all the good and great were continual sins and perpetual crimes; that the love a mother bears her child is, in the sight of god, a sin; that the gratitude of the natural heart is simple meanness; that the tears of pity are impure; that for the unconverted to live and labor for others is an offense to heaven; that the noblest aspirations of the soul are low and groveling in the sight of God; that man should fall upon his knees and ask forgiveness, simply for loving his wife and child; and that even the act of asking forgiveness is in fact a crime!

Surely it is a kind of bliss to feel that every woman and child in the wide world, with the exception of those who believe the five points, or some other equally cruel creed, and such children as have been baptized, ought at this very moment to be dashed down to the lowest glowing gulf of hell.

Take from the Christian the history of his own church—leave that entirely out of the question—and he has no argument left with which to substantiate the total depravity of man.

Eleventh. With having doubted the "perseverance of the saints."

I suppose the real meaning of this doctrine is that Presbyterians are just as sure of going to heaven as all other folks are of going to hell. The real idea being that it all depends upon the will of God, and not upon the character of the person to be damned or saved; that God has the weakness to send Presbyterians to Paradise, and the justice to doom the rest of mankind to eternal fire.

It is admitted that no unconverted brain can see the least particle of sense in this doctrine; that it is abhorrent to all who have not been the recipients of a "new heart"; that only the perfectly good can justify the perfectly infamous.

It is contended that the saints do not persevere of their own free will—that they are entitled to no credit for persevering; but that God forces them to persevere, while on the other hand every crime is committed in accordance with the secret will of God, who does all things for his own glory.

Compared with this doctrine, there is no other idea, that has ever been believed by man, that can properly be called absurd.

Twelfth. With having spoken and written somewhat lightly of the idea of converting the heathen with doctrinal sermons.

Of all the failures of which we have any history or knowledge, the missionary effort is the most conspicuous. The whole question has been decided here, in our own country, and conclusively settled. We have nearly exterminated the Indians, but we have converted none. From the days of John Eliot to the execution of the last Modoc, not one Indian has been the subject of irresistible grace or particular redemption. The few red men who roam the western wilderness have no thought or care concerning the five points of Calvin. They are utterly oblivious to the great and vital truths contained in the Thirty-nine Articles, the Saybrook platform, and the resolutions of the Evangelical Alliance. No Indian has ever scalped another on account of his religious belief. This of itself shows conclusively that the missionaries have had no effect.

Why should we convert the heathen of China and kill our own? Why should we send missionaries across the seas, and soldiers over the plains? Why should we send Bibles to the east and muskets to the west? If it is impossible to convert Indians who have no religion of their own, no prejudice for or against the "eternal procession of the Holy Ghost," how can we expect to convert a heathen who has a religion; who has plenty of gods and Bibles and prophets and Christs, and who has a religious literature far grander than our own? Can we hope with the story of Daniel in the lions' den to rival the stupendous miracles of India? Is there anything in our Bible as lofty and loving as the prayer of the Buddhist? Compare your "Confession of Faith" with the following: "Never will I seek nor receive private individual salvation—never enter into final peace alone; but forever and everywhere will I live and strive for the universal redemption of every creature throughout all worlds. Until all are delivered, never will I leave the world of sin, sorrow, and struggle, but will remain where I am."

Think of sending an average Presbyterian to convert a man

who daily offers this tender, this infinitely generous, this incomparable prayer. Think of reading the 109th Psalm to a heathen who has a Bible of his own in which is found this passage: "Blessed is that man and beloved of all the gods, who is afraid of no man, and of whom no man is afraid."

Why should you read even the New Testament to a Hindu, when his own Chrishna has said, "If a man strike thee, and in striking drop his staff, pick it up and hand it to him again"? Why send a Presbyterian to a Sufi, who says, "Better one moment of silent contemplation and inward love, than seventy thousand years of outward worship"? "Whoso would carelessly tread one worm that crawls on earth, that heartless one is darkly alienate from God; but he that, living, embraceth all things in his love, to live with him God bursts all bounds above, below."

Why should we endeavor to thrust our cruel and heartless theology upon one who prays this prayer: "O God, show pity toward the wicked; for on the good thou hast already bestowed thy mercy by having created them virtuous"?

Compare this prayer with the curses and cruelties of the Old Testament—with the infamies commanded and approved by the being whom we are taught to worship as a god—and with the following tender product of Presbyterianism: "It may seem absurd to human wisdom that God should harden, blind, and deliver up some men to a reprobate sense; that he should first deliver them over to evil, and then condemn them for that evil; but the believing spiritual man sees no absurdity in all this, knowing that God would be never a whit less good even though he should destroy all men."

Of all the religions that have been produced by the egotism, the malice, the ignorance, and ambition of man, Presbyterianism is the most hideous.

But what shall I say more, for the time would fail me to tell of Sabellianism, of a "Modal Trinity," and the "Eternal Procession of the Holy Ghost"?

Upon these charges, a minister is to be tried, here in Chicago; in this city of pluck and progress—this marvel of energy—this miracle of nerve. The cry of "heresy," here, sounds like a wail from the Dark Ages—a shriek from the Inquisition, or a groan from the grave of Calvin.

Another effort is being made to enslave a man.

It is claimed that every member of the church has solemnly agreed never to outgrow the creed; that he has pledged himself to remain an intellectual dwarf. Upon this condition the church agrees to save his soul, and he hands over his brains to bind the bargain. Should a fact be found inconsistent with the creed, he binds himself to deny the fact and curse the finder. With scraps of dogmas and crumbs of doctrine, he agrees that his soul shall be satisfied forever. What an intellectual feast the Confession of Faith must be! It reminds one of the dinner described by Sydney Smith, where everything was cold except the water, and everything sour except the vinegar.

Every member of a church promises to remain orthodox, that is to say—stationary. Growth is heresy. Orthodox ideas are the feathers that have been molted by the eagle of progress. They are the dead leaves under the majestic palm, while heresy is the bud and blossom at the top.

Imagine a vine that grows at one end and decays at the other. The end that grows is heresy, the end that rots is orthodox. The dead are orthodox, and your cemetery is the most perfect type of a well-regulated church. No thought, no progress, no heresy there. Slowly and silently, side by side, the satisfied members peacefully decay. There is only this difference—the dead do not persecute.

And what does a trial for heresy mean? It means that the church says to a heretic, "Believe as I do, or I will withdraw my support. I will not employ you. I will pursue you until your garments are rags; until your children cry for bread; until your cheeks are furrowed with tears. I will hunt you to the very portals of the tomb, and then my God will do the rest. I will not imprison you. I will not burn you. The law prevents my doing that. I helped make the law, not however to protect you, nor to deprive me of the right to exterminate you, but in order to keep other churches from exterminating me."

A trial for heresy means that the spirit of persecution still lingers in the church; that it still denies the right of private judgment; that it still thinks more of creed than truth; and that it is still determined to prevent the intellectual growth of man. It means that churches are shambles in which are bought and sold the souls of men. It means that the church is still guilty of the barbarity of opposing thought with force. It means that if it had the power, the mental horizon would be bounded by a creed; that it would bring again the whips and chains and dungeon keys, the rack and fagot of the past.

But let me tell the church it lacks the power. There have been, and still are, too many men who own themselves—too much thought, too much knowledge for the church to grasp again the sword of power. The church must abdicate. For the Eglon of superstition Science has a message from Truth.

The heretics have not thought and suffered and died in vain. Every heretic has been, and is, a ray of light. Not in vain did Voltaire, that great man, point from the foot of the Alps the finger of scorn at every hypocrite in Europe. Not in vain were the splendid utterances of the infidels, while beyond all price are the discoveries of science.

The church has impeded, but it has not and it cannot stop the onward march of the human race. Heresy cannot be burned, nor imprisoned, nor starved. It laughs at presbyteries and synods, at ecumenical councils and the impotent thunders of Sinai. Heresy is the eternal dawn, the morning star, the glittering herald of the day. Heresy is the last and best thought. It is the perpetual New World, the unknown sea, toward which the brave all sail. It is the eternal horizon of progress.

Heresy extends the hospitalities of the brain to a new thought.

Heresy is a cradle; orthodoxy, a coffin.

Why should man be afraid to think, and why should he fear to express his thoughts?

Is it possible that an infinite Deity is unwilling that a man should investigate the phenomena by which he is surrounded? Is it possible that a god delights in threatening and terrifying men? What glory, what honor and renown a god must win on such a field! The ocean raving at a drop; a star envious of a candle; the sun jealous of a firefly.

Go on, presbyteries and synods, go on! Thrust the heretics out of the church—that is to say, throw away your brains,—put out your eyes. The infidels will thank you. They are willing to adopt your exiles. Every deserter from your camp is a recruit for the army of progress. Cling to the ignorant dogmas of the past; read the 109th Psalm; gloat over the slaughter of mothers and babes; thank God for total depravity; shower your honors upon hypocrites; and silence every minister who is touched with that heresy called genius.

Be true to your history. Turn out the astronomers, the geologists, the naturalists, the chemists, and all the honest scientists. With a whip of scorpions, drive them all out. We want them all. Keep the ignorant, the superstitious, the bigoted, and the writers of charges and specifications. Keep them, and keep them all. Repeat your pious platitudes in the drowsy ears of the faithful, and read your Bible to heretics, as kings read some forgotten riot act to stop and stay the waves of revolution. You are too weak to excite anger. We forgive your efforts as the sun forgives a cloud—as the air forgives the breath you waste.

How long, O how long, will man listen to the threats of God, and shut his eyes to the splendid possibilities of Nature? How long, O how long will man remain the cringing slave of a false and cruel creed?

By this time the whole world should know that the real Bible has not yet been written, but is being written, and that it will never be finished until the race begins its downward march, or ceases to exist.

The real Bible is not the work of inspired men, nor prophets, nor apostles, nor evangelists, nor of Christs. Every man who finds a fact adds, as it were, a word to this great book. It is not attested by prophecy, by miracles, or signs. It makes no appeal to faith, to ignorance, to credulity, or fear. It has no punishment for unbelief, and no reward for hypocrisy. It appeals to man in the name of demonstration. It has nothing to conceal. It has no fear of being read, of being contradicted, of being investigated and understood. It does not pretend to be holy, or sacred; it simply claims to be true. It challenges the scrutiny of all, and implores every reader to verify every line for himself. It is incapable of being blasphemed. This book appeals to all the surroundings of man. Each thing that exists testifies of its perfection. The earth, with its heart of fire and crowns of snow; with its forests and plains, its rocks and seas; with its every wave and cloud; with its every leaf and bud and flower, confirms its every word, and the solemn stars, shining in the infinite abysses, are the eternal witnesses of its truth.

THE GHOSTS

PREFACE

These lectures have been so maimed and mutilated by orthodox malice; have been made to appear so halt, crutched, and decrepit by those who mistake the pleasures of calumny for the duties of religion, that in simple justice to myself I concluded to publish them.

Most of the clergy are, or seem to be, utterly incapable of discussing anything in a fair and catholic spirit. They appeal, not to reason, but to prejudice; not to facts, but to passages of Scripture. They can conceive of no goodness, of no spiritual exaltation beyond the horizon of their creed. Whoever differs with them upon what they are pleased to call "fundamental truths" is, in their opinion, a base and infamous man. To reenact the tragedies of the sixteenth century, they lack only the power. Bigotry in all ages has been the same. Christianity simply transferred the brutality of the Colosseum to the Inquisition. For the murderous combat of the gladiators, the saints substituted the *auto de fé*. What has been called religion is, after all, but the organization of the wild beast in man. The perfumed blossom of arrogance is heaven. Hell is the consummation of revenge.

The chief business of the clergy has always been to destroy the joy of life, and multiply and magnify the terrors and tortures of death and perdition. They have polluted the heart and paralyzed the brain; and upon the ignorant altars of the Past and the Dead, they have endeavored to sacrifice the Present and the Living.

Nothing can exceed the mendacity of the religious press. I have had some little experience with political editors, and am forced to say that until I read the religious papers, I did not know what malicious and slimy falsehoods could be constructed from ordinary words. The ingenuity with which the real and apparent meaning can be tortured out of language is simply amazing. The average religious editor is intolerant and insolent; he knows nothing of affairs; he has the envy of failure, the malice of impotence, and always accounts for the brave and generous actions of unbelievers by low, base, and unworthy motives.

By this time, even the clergy should know that the intellect of the nineteenth century needs no guardian. They should cease to regard themselves as shepherds defending flocks of weak, silly, and fearful sheep from the claws and teeth of ravening wolves. By this time they should know that the religion of the ignorant and brutal Past no longer satisfies the heart and brain; that the miracles have become contemptible; that the "evidences" have ceased to convince; that the spirit of investigation cannot be stopped nor stayed; that the church is losing her power; that the young are holding in a kind of tender contempt the sacred follies of the old; that the pulpit and pews no longer represent the culture and morality of the world; and that the brand of intellectual inferiority is upon the orthodox brain.

Men should be liberated from the aristocracy of the air. Every chain of superstition should be broken. The rights of men and women should be equal and sacred—marriage should be a perfect partnership—children should be governed by kindness,—every family should be a republic—every fireside a democracy.

It seems almost impossible for religious people to really grasp the idea of intellectual freedom. They seem to think that man is responsible for his honest thoughts, that unbelief is a crime, that investigation is sinful, that credulity is a virtue, and that reason is a dangerous guide. They cannot divest themselves of the idea that in the realm of thought there must be government—authority and obedience—laws and penalties—rewards and punishments, and that somewhere in the universe there is a penitentiary for the soul.

In the republic of mind, *one* is a majority. There, all are monarchs, and all are equals. The tyranny of a majority even is unknown. Each one is crowned, sceptered, and throned. Upon every brow is the tiara, and around every form is the imperial purple. Only those are good citizens who express their honest thoughts, and those who persecute for opinion's sake are the only traitors. There, nothing is considered infamous except an appeal to brute force, and nothing sacred but love, liberty, and joy. The church contemplates this republic with a sneer. From the teeth of hatred she draws back the lips of scorn. She is filled with the spite and spleen born of intellectual weakness. Once she was egotistic; now she is envious. Once she wore upon her hollow breast false gems, supposing them to be real. They have been shown to be false, but she wears them still. She has the malice of the caught, the hatred of the exposed.

We are told to investigate the Bible for ourselves, and at the same time informed that if we come to the conclusion that it is not the inspired word of God, we will most assuredly be damned. Under such circumstances, if we believe this, investigation is impossible. Whoever is held responsible for his conclusions cannot weigh the evidence with impartial scales. Fear stands at the balance, and gives to falsehood the weight of its trembling hand.

I oppose the church because she is the enemy of liberty; because her dogmas are infamous and cruel; because she humiliates and degrades woman; because she teaches the doctrines of eternal torment and the natural depravity of man; because she insists upon the absurd, the impossible, and the senseless; because she resorts to falsehood and slander; because she is arrogant and revengeful; because she allows men to sin on a credit; because she discourages self-reliance, and laughs at good works; because she believes in vacarious virtue and vicarious vice—vicarious punishment and vicarious reward; because she regards repentance of more importance than restitution; and because she sacrifices the world we have to one we know not of.

The free and generous, the tender and affectionate, will understand me. Those who have escaped from the grated cells of a creed will appreciate my motives. The sad and suffering wives, the trembling and loving children will thank me: This is enough.

ROBERT G. INGERSOLL

WASHINGTON, D.C.,
APRIL 13, 1878

THE GHOSTS

LET THEM COVER THEIR EYELESS SOCKETS
WITH THEIR FLESHLESS HANDS AND FADE FOREVER
FROM THE IMAGINATION OF MEN

There are three theories by which men account for all phenomena, for everything that happens: first, the Supernatural; second, the Supernatural and Natural; third, the Natural. Between these theories there has been, from the dawn of civilization, a continual conflict. In this great war, nearly all the soldiers have been in the ranks of the supernatural. The believers in the supernatural insist that matter is controlled and directed entirely by powers from without; while naturalists maintain that Nature acts from within, that Nature is not acted upon, that the universe is all there is, that Nature with infinite arms embraces everything that exists, and that all supposed powers beyond the limits of the material are simply ghosts. You say, "Oh, this is materialism!" What is matter? I take in my hand some earth:—in this dust put seeds. Let the arrows of light from the quiver of the sun smite upon it; let the rain fall upon it. The seeds will grow and a plant will bud and blossom. Do you understand this? Can you explain it better than you can the production of thought? Have you the

143

slightest conception of what it really is? And yet you speak of matter as though acquainted with its origin, as though you had torn from the clenched hands of the rocks the secrets of material existence. Do you know what force is? Can you account for molecular action? Are you really familiar with chemistry, and can you account for the loves and hatreds of the atoms? Is there not something in matter that forever eludes? After all, can you get beyond, above, or below appearances? Before you cry "materialism!" had you not better ascertain what matter really is? Can you think even of anything without a material basis? Is it possible to imagine the annihilation of a single atom? Is it possible for you to conceive of the creation of an atom? Can you have a thought that was not suggested to you by what you call matter?

Our fathers denounced materialism, and accounted for all phenomena by the caprice of gods and devils.

For thousands of years it was believed that ghosts, good and bad, benevolent and malignant, weak and powerful, in some mysterious way, produced all phenomena; that disease and health, happiness and misery, fortune and misfortune, peace and war, life and death, success and failure, were but arrows from the quivers of these ghosts; that shadowy phantoms rewarded and punished mankind; that they were pleased and displeased by the actions of men; that they sent and withheld the snow, the light, and the rain; that they blessed the earth with harvests or cursed it with famine; that they fed or starved the children of men; that they crowned and uncrowned kings; that they took sides in war; that they controlled the winds; that they gave prosperous voyages, allowing the brave mariner to meet his wife and child inside the harbor bar; or sent the storms, strewing the sad shores with wrecks of ships and the bodies of men.

Formerly, these ghosts were believed to be almost innumerable. Earth, air, and water were filled with these phantom hosts. In modern times they have greatly decreased in number, because the second theory—a mingling of the supernatural and natural—has generally been adopted. The remaining ghosts, however, are supposed to perform the same offices as the hosts of yore.

It has always been believed that these ghosts could in some way be appeased; that they could be flattered by sacrifices, by prayer, by fasting, by the building of temples and cathedrals, by the blood of men and beasts, by forms and ceremonies, by chants, by kneelings and prostrations, by flagellations and maimings, by renouncing the joys of home, by living alone in the wide desert, by the practice of celibacy, by inventing instruments of torture, by destroying men, women, and children, by covering the earth with dungeons, by burning unbelievers, by putting chains upon the thoughts and manacles upon the limbs of men, by believing things without evidence and against evidence, by disbelieving and denying demonstration, by despising facts, by hating reason, by denouncing liberty, by maligning heretics, by slandering the dead, by subscribing to senseless and cruel creeds, by discouraging investigation, by worshiping a book, by the cultivation of credulity, by observing certain times and days, by counting beads, by gazing at crosses, by hiring others to repeat verses and prayers, by burning candles and ringing bells, by enslaving each other and putting out the eyes of the soul. All this has been done to appease and flatter these monsters of the air.

In the history of our poor world, no horror has been omitted, no infamy has been left undone by the believers in ghosts,—by the worshipers of these fleshless phantoms. And yet these shadows were born of cowardice and malignity. They were painted by the pencil of fear upon the canvas of ignorance by that artist called superstition.

From these ghosts, our fathers received information. They were the schoolmasters of our ancestors. They were the scientists and philosophers, the geologists, legislators, astronomers, physicians, metaphysicians, and historians of the past. For ages these ghosts were supposed to be the only source of real knowledge. They inspired men to write books, and the books were considered sacred. If facts were found to be inconsistent with these books, so much the worse for the facts, and especially for their discoverers. It was then, and still is, believed that these books are the basis of the idea of immortaility; that to give up these volumes, or rather the idea that they are inspired, is to renounce the idea of immortality. This I deny.

The idea of immortality, that like a sea has ebbed and flowed in the human heart, with its countless waves of hope and fear, beating against the shores and rocks of time and fate, was not born of any book, nor of any creed, nor of any religion. It was born of human affection, and it will continue to ebb and flow beneath the mists and clouds of doubt and darkness as long as love kisses the lips of death. It is the rainbow—Hope shining upon the tears of grief.

From the books written by the ghosts we have at last ascertained that they knew nothing about the world in which we live. Did they know anything about the next? Upon every point where contradiction is possible, they have been contradicted.

By these ghosts, by these citizens of the air, the affairs of government were administered; all authority to govern came from them. The emperors, kings, and potentates all had commissions from these phantoms. Man was not considered as the source of any power whatever. To rebel against the king was to rebel against the ghosts, and nothing less than the blood of the offender could appease the invisible phantom or the visible tyrant. Kneeling was the proper position to be assumed by the multitude. The prostrate were the good. Those who stood erect were infidels and traitors. In the name and by the authority of the ghosts, man was enslaved, crushed, and plundered. The many toiled wearily in the storm and sun that the few favorites of the ghosts might live in idleness. The many lived in huts, and caves, and dens, that the few might dwell in palaces. The many covered themselves with rags, that the few might robe themselves in purple and gold. The many crept, and cringed, and crawled, that the few might tread upon their flesh with iron feet.

From the ghosts men received not only authority, but information of every kind. They told us the form of this earth. They informed us that eclipses were caused by the sins of man;

that the universe was made in six days; that astronomy and geology were devices of wicked men, instigated by wicked ghosts; that gazing at the sky with a telescope was a dangerous thing; that digging into the earth was sinful curiosity; that trying to be wise above what they had written was born of a rebellious and irreverent spirit.

They told us there was no virtue like belief, and no crime like doubt; that investigation was pure impudence, and the punishment therefor, eternal torment. They not only told us all about this world, but about two others; and if their statements about the other worlds are as true as about this, no one can estimate the value of their information.

For countless ages the world was governed by ghosts, and they spared no pains to change the eagle of human intellect into a bat of darkness. To accomplish this infamous purpose; to drive the love of truth from the human heart; to prevent the advancement of mankind; to shut out from the world every ray of intellectual light; to pollute every mind with superstition, the power of kings, the cunning and cruelty of priests, and the wealth of nations were exhausted.

During these years of persecution, ignorance, superstition, and slavery, nearly all the people, the kings, lawyers, doctors, the learned and the unlearned, believed in that frightful production of ignorance, fear, and faith called witchcraft. They believed that man was the sport and prey of devils. They really thought that the very air was thick with these enemies of man. With few exceptions, this hideous and infamous belief was universal. Under these conditions, progress was almost impossible.

Fear paralyzes the brain. Progress is born of courage. Fear believes—courage doubts. Fear falls upon the earth and prays— courage stands erect and thinks. Fear retreats—courage advances. Fear is barbarism—courage is civilization. Fear believes in witchcraft, in devils, and in ghosts. Fear is religion—courage is science.

The facts, upon which this terrible belief rested, were probed over and over again in every court of Europe. Thousands confessed themselves guilty—admitted that they had sold themselves to the devil. They gave the particulars of the sale; told what they said and what the devil replied. They confessed this, when they knew that confession was death; knew that their property would be confiscated, and their children left to beg their bread. This is one of the miracles of history—one of the strangest contradictions of the human mind. Without doubt, they really believed themselves guilty. In the first place, they believed in witchcraft as a fact, and when charged with it, they probably became insane. In their insanity they confessed their guilt. They found themselves abhorred and deserted—charged with a crime that they could not disprove. Like a man in quicksand, every effort only sunk them deeper. Caught in this frightful web, at the mercy of the spiders of superstition, hope fled, and nothing remained but the insanity of confession. The whole world appeared to be insane.

In the time of James the First, a man was executed for causing a storm at sea with the intention of drowning one of the royal family. How could he disprove it? How could he show that he did not cause the storm? All storms were at that time generally supposed to be caused by the devil—the prince of the power of the air—and by those whom he assisted.

I implore you to remember that the believers in such impossible things were the authors of our creeds and confessions of faith.

A woman was tried and convicted before Sir Matthew Hale, one of the great judges and lawyers of England, for having caused children to vomit crooked pins. She was also charged with having nursed devils. The learned judge charged the intelligent jury that there was no doubt as to the existence of witches; that it was established by all history, and expressly taught by the Bible.

The woman was hanged and her body burned.

Sir Thomas More declared that to give up witchcraft was to throw away the sacred Scriptures. In my judgment, he was right.

John Wesley was a firm believer in ghosts and witches, and insisted upon it, years after all laws upon the subject had been repealed in England. I beg of you to remember that John Wesley was the founder of the Methodist Church.

In New England, a woman was charged with being a witch, and with having changed herself into a fox. While in that condition she was attacked and bitten by some dogs. A commitee of three men, by order of the court, examined this woman. They removed her clothing and searched for "witch spots." That is to say, spots into which needles could be thrust without giving her pain. They reported to the court that such spots were found. She denied, however, that she ever had changed herself into a fox. Upon the report of the committee she was found guilty and actually executed. This was done by our Puritan fathers, by the gentlemen who braved the dangers of the deep for the sake of worshiping God and persecuting their fellowmen.

In those days people believed in what was known as lycan-thropy—that is, that persons, with the assistance of the devil, could assume the form of wolves. An instance is given where a man was attacked by a wolf. He defended himself, and succeeded in cutting off one of the animal's paws. The wolf ran away. The man picked up the paw, put it in his pocket and carried it home. There he found his wife with one of her hands gone. He took the paw from his pocket. It had changed to a human hand. He charged his wife with being a witch. She was tried. She confessed her guilt, and was burned.

People were burned for causing frosts in summer—for destroying crops with hail—for causing storms—for making cows go dry, and even for souring beer. There was no impossibility for which some one was not tried and convicted. The life of no one was secure. To be charged was to be convicted. Every man was at the mercy of every other. This infamous belief was so firmly seated in the minds of the people that to express a doubt as to its truth was to be suspected. Whoever denied the existence of witches and devils was denounced as an infidel.

They believed that animals were often taken possession of by devils, and that the killing of the animal would destroy the devil. They absolutely tried, convicted, and executed dumb beasts.

At Basle, in 1470, a rooster was tried upon the charge of having laid an egg. Rooster eggs were used only in making witch ointment,—this everybody knew. The rooster was convicted and with all due solemnity was burned in the public square. So a hog and six pigs were tried for having killed and partially eaten a child. The hog was convicted,—but the pigs, on account probably of their extreme youth, were acquitted. As late as 1740, a cow was tried and convicted of being possessed by a devil.

They used to exorcise rats, locusts, snakes, and vermin. They used to go through the alleys, streets, and fields, and warn them to leave within a certain number of days. In case they disobeyed, they were threatened with pains and penalties.

But let us be careful how we laugh at these things. Let us not pride ourselves too much on the progress of our age. We must not forget that some of our people are yet in the same intelligent business. Only a little while ago, the governor of Minnesota appointed a day of fasting and prayer, to see if some power could not be induced to kill the grasshoppers, or send them into some other state.

About the close of the fifteenth century, so great was the excitement with regard to the existence of witchcraft that Pope Innocent VIII issued a bull directing the inquisitors to be vigilant in searching out and punishing all guilty of this crime. Forms for the trial were regularly laid down in a book or a pamphlet called the "MALLEUS MALEFICORUM" (Hammer of Witches), which was issued by the Roman See. Popes Alexander, Leo, and Adrian issued like bulls. For two hundred and fifty years the church was busy in punishing the impossible crime of witchcraft; in burning, hanging, and torturing men, women, and children. Protestants were as active as Catholics, and in Geneva five hundred witches were burned at the stake in a period of three months. About one thousand were executed in one year in the diocese of Como. At least one hundred thousand victims suffered in Germany alone: the last execution (in Wurtzburg) taking place as late as 1749. Witches were burned in Switzerland as late as 1780.

In England the same frightful scenes were enacted. Statutes were passed from Henry VI to James I, defining the crime and its punishment. The last act passed by the British parliament was when Lord Bacon was a member of the House of Commons; and this act was not repealed until 1736.

Sir William Blackstone, in his Commentaries on the Laws of England, says: "To deny the possibility, nay, actual existence of witchcraft and sorcery, is at once flatly to contradict the word of God in various passages both of the Old and New Testament; and the thing itself is a truth to which every nation in the world hath in its turn borne testimony, either by examples seemingly well attested, or by prohibitory laws, which at least suppose the possibility of a commerce with evil spirits."

In Brown's Dictionary of the Bible, published at Edinburg, Scotland, in 1807, it is said that: "A witch is a woman that has dealings with Satan. That such persons are among men is abundantly plain from Scripture, and that they ought to be put to death."

This work was republished in Albany, New York, in 1816. No wonder the clergy of that city are ignorant and bigoted even unto this day.

In 1716, Mrs. Hicks and her daughter, nine years of age, were hanged for selling their souls to the devil, and raising a storm by pulling off their stockings and making a lather of soap.

In England it has been estimated that at least thirty thousand were hanged and burned. The last victim executed in Scotland perished in 1722. "She was an innocent old woman, who had so little idea of her situation as to rejoice at the sight of the fire which was destined to consume her. She had a daughter, lame both of hands and of feet—a circumstance attributed to the witch having been used to transform her daughter into a pony and getting her shod by the devil."

In 1692, nineteen persons were executed and one pressed to death in Salem, Massachusetts, for the crime of witchcraft.

It was thought in those days that men and women made compacts with the devil, orally and in writing. That they abjured God and Jesus Christ, and dedicated themselves wholly to the devil. The contracts were confirmed at a general meeting of witches and ghosts, over which the devil himself presided; and the persons generally signed the articles of agreement with their own blood. These contracts were, in some instances, for a few years; in others, for life. General assemblies of the witches were held at least once a year, at which they appeared entirely naked, besmeared with an ointment made from the bodies of unbaptized infants. "To these meetings they rode from great distances on broomsticks, pokers, goats, hogs, and dogs. Here they did homage to the prince of hell, and offered him sacrifices of young children, and practiced all sorts of license until the break of day."

"As late as 1815, Belgium was disgraced by a witch trial; and guilt was established by the water ordeal." "In 1836, the populace of Hela, near Dantzic, twice plunged into the sea a woman reputed to be a sorceress; and as the miserable creature persisted in rising to the surface, she was pronounced guilty, and beaten to death."

"It was believed that the bodies of devils are not like those of men and animals, cast in an unchangeable mold. It was thought they were like clouds, refined and subtle matter, capable of assuming any form and penetrating into any orifice. The horrible tortures they endured in their place of punishment rendered them extremely sensitive to suffering, and they continually sought a temperate and somewhat moist warmth in order to allay their pangs. It was for this reason they so frequently entered into men and women."

The devil could transport men, at his will, through the air. He could beget children; and Martin Luther himself had come in contact with one of these children. He recommended the mother to throw the child into the river, in order to free their house from the presence of a devil.

It was believed that the devil could transform people into any shape he pleased.

Whoever denied these things was denounced as an infidel. All the believers in witchcraft confidently appealed to the Bible. Their mouths were filled with passages demonstrating the existence of witches and their power over human beings. By the Bible they proved that innumerable evil spirits were ranging over the world endeavoring to ruin mankind; that these spirits possessed a power and wisdom far transcending the limits of human faculties; that they delighted in every misfortune that could befall the world; that their malice was superhuman. That they caused tempests was proved by the action of the devil toward Job; by the passage in the book of Revelation describing the four angels who held the four winds, and to whom it was given to afflict the earth. They believed the devil could carry persons hundreds of miles, in a few seconds, through the air. They believed this, because they knew that Christ had been carried by the devil in the same manner and placed on a pinnacle of the temple. "The prophet Habakkuk had been transported by a spirit from Judea to Babylon; and Philip, the evangelist, had been the object of a similar miracle; and in the same way Saint Paul had been carried in the body into the third heaven."

"In those pious days, they believed that *incubi* and *succubi* were forever wandering among mankind, alluring, by more than human charms, the unwary to their destruction, and laying plots, which were too often successful, against the virtue of the saints. Sometimes the witches kindled in the monastic priest a more terrestrial fire. People told, with bated breath, how, under the spell of a vindictive woman, four successive abbots in a German monastery had been wasted away by an unholy flame."

An instance is given in which the devil not only assumed the appearance of a holy man, in order to pay his addresses to a lady, but when discovered, crept under the bed, suffered himself to be dragged out, and was impudent enough to declare that he was the veritable bishop. So perfectly had he assumed the form and features of the prelate that those who knew the bishop best were deceived.

One can hardly imagine the frightful state of the human mind during these long centuries of darkness and superstition. To them, these things were awful and frightening realities. Hovering above them in the air, in their houses, in the bosoms of friends, in their very bodies, in all the darkness of night, everywhere, around, above and below, were innumerable hosts of unclean and malignant devils.

From the malice of those leering and vindictive vampires of the air, the church pretended to defend mankind. Pursued by these phantoms, the frightened multitudes fell upon their faces and implored the aid of robed hypocrisy and sceptered theft.

Take from the orthodox church today the threat and fear of hell, and it becomes an extinct volcano.

Take from the church the miraculous, the supernatural, the incomprehensible, the unreasonable, the impossible, the unknowable, and the absurd, and nothing but a vacuum remains.

Notwithstanding all the infamous things justly laid to the charge of the church, we are told that the civilization of today is the child of what we are pleased to call the superstition of the past.

Religion has not civilized man—man has civilized religion. God improves as man advances.

Let me call your attention to what we have received from the followers of the ghosts. Let me give you an outline of the sciences as taught by these philosophers of the clouds.

All diseases were produced, either as a punishment by the good ghosts, or out of pure malignity by the bad ones. There were, properly speaking, no diseases. The sick were possessed by ghosts. The science of medicine consisted in knowing how to persuade these ghosts to vacate the premises. For thousands of years the diseased were treated with incantations, with hideous noises, with drums and gongs. Everything was done to make the visit of the ghost as unpleasant as possible, and they generally succeeded in making things so disagreeable that if the ghost did not leave, the patient did. These ghosts were supposed to be of different rank, power, and dignity. Now and then a man pretended to have won the favor of some powerful ghost, and that gave him power over the little ones. Such a man became an eminent physician.

It was found that certain kinds of smoke, such as that produced by burning the liver of a fish, the dried skin of a serpent, the eyes of a toad, or the tongue of an adder, were exceedingly offensive to the nostrils of an ordinary ghost. With this smoke, the sick room would be filled until the ghost vanished or the patient died.

It was also believed that certain words—the names of the most powerful ghosts—when properly pronounced, were very effective weapons. It was for a long time thought that Latin words were the best,—Latin being a dead language, and known by the clergy. Others thought that two sticks laid across each other and held before the wicked ghost would cause it instantly to flee in dread away.

For thousands of years, the practice of medicine consisted in driving these evil spirits out of the bodies of men.

In some instances, bargains and compromises were made with the ghosts. One case is given where a multitude of devils traded a man for a herd of swine. In this transaction the devils were the losers, as the swine immediately drowned themselves in the sea. This idea of disease appears to have been almost universal, and is by no means yet extinct.

The contortions of the epileptic, the strange twitchings of those afflicted with chorea, the shakings of palsy, dreams, trances, and the numberless frightful phenomena produced by diseases of the nerves, were all seized upon as so many proofs that the bodies of men were filled with unclean and malignant ghosts.

Whoever endeavored to account for these things by natural causes, whoever attempted to cure diseases by natural means, was denounced by the church as an infidel. To explain anything was a crime. It was to the interest of the priest that all phenomena should be accounted for by the will and power of gods and devils. The moment it is admitted that all phenomena are within the domain of the natural, the necessity for a priest has disappeared.

Religion breathes the air of the supernatural. Take from the mind of man the idea of the supernatural, and religion ceases to exist. For this reason, the church has always despised the man who explained the wonderful. Upon this principle, nothing was left undone to stay the science of medicine. As long as plagues and pestilences could be stopped by prayer, the priest was useful. The moment the physician found a cure, the priest became an extravagance. The moment it began to be apparent that prayer could do nothing for the body, the priest shifted his ground and began praying for the soul.

Long after the devil idea was substantially abandoned in the practice of medicine, and when it was admitted that God had nothing to do with ordinary coughs and colds, it was still believed that all the frightful diseases were sent by him as punishments for the wickedness of the people. It was thought to be a kind of blasphemy to even try, by any natural means, to stay the ravages of pestilence. Formerly, during the prevalence of plague and epidemics, the arrogance of the priest was boundless. He told the people that they had slighted the clergy, that they had refused to pay tithes, that they had doubted some of the doctrines of the church, and that God was now taking his revenge. The people for the most part believed this infamous tissue of priestcraft. They hastened to fall upon their knees; they poured out their wealth upon the altars of hypocrisy; they abased and debased themselves; from their minds they banished all doubts, and made haste to crawl in the very dust of humility.

The church never wanted disease to be under the control of man. Timothy Dwight, president of Yale College, preached a sermon against vaccination. His idea was that if God had decreed from all eternity that a certain man should die with the smallpox, it was a frightful sin to avoid and annul that decree by the trick of vaccination. Smallpox being regarded as one of the heaviest guns in the arsenal of heaven, to spike it was the height of presumption. Plagues and pestilences were instrumentalities in the hands of God with which to gain the love and worship of mankind.

To find a cure for disease was to take a weapon from the church. No one tries to cure the ague with prayer. Quinine has been found altogether more reliable. Just as soon as a specific is found for a disease, that disease will be left out of the list of prayer. The number of diseases with which God from time to time afflicts mankind is continually decreasing. In a few years all of them will be under the control of man, the gods will be left unarmed, and the threats of their priests will excite only a smile.

The science of medicine has had but one enemy—religion. Man was afraid to save his body for fear he might lose his soul.

Is it any wonder that the people in those days believed in and taught the infamous doctrine of eternal punishment—a doctrine that makes God a heartless monster and man a slimy hypocrite and slave?

The ghosts were historians, and their histories were the grossest absurdities. "Tales told by idiots, full of sound and fury, signifying nothing." In those days the histories were written by the monks, who, as a rule, were almost as superstitious as they were dishonest. They wrote as though they had been witnesses of every occurrence they related. They wrote the history of every country of importance. They told all the past and predicted all the future with an impudence that amounted to sublimity. "They traced the order of St. Michael, in France, to the archangel himself, and alleged that he was the founder of a chivalric order in heaven itself. They said that Tartars originally came from hell, and that they were called Tartars because Tartarus was one of the names of perdition. They declared that Scotland was so named after Scota, a daughter of Pharaoh, who landed in Ireland, invaded Scotland, and took it by force of arms. This statement was made in a letter addressed to the Pope in the fourteenth century, and was alluded to as a well-known fact. The letter was written by some of the highest dignitaries, and by the direction of the King himself."

These gentlemen accounted for the red on the breasts of robins from the fact that these birds carried water to unbaptized infants in hell.

Matthew, of Paris, an eminent historian of the fourteenth century, gave the world the following piece of information: "It is well known that Mohammed was once a cardinal, and became a heretic because he failed in his effort to be elected pope"; and that having drunk to excess, he fell by the roadside, and in this condition was killed by swine. "And for that reason, his followers abhor pork even unto this day."

Another eminent historian informs us that Nero was in the habit of vomiting frogs. When I read this, I said to myself: Some of the croakers of the present day against Progress would be the better for such a vomit.

The history of Charlemagne was written by Turpin, of Rheims. He was a bishop. He assures us that the walls of a city fell down in answer to prayer. That there were giants in those days who could take fifty ordinary men under their arms and walk away with them. "With the greatest of ease, a direct descendant of Goliath, one Orlando had a theological discussion, and that in the heat of the debate, when the giant was overwhelmed with the argument, Orlando rushed forward and inflicted a fatal stab."

The history of Britain, written by the archdeacons of Monmouth and Oxford, was wonderfully popular. According to them, Brutus conquered England and built the city of London. During his time, it rained pure blood for three days. At another time, a monster came from the sea, and, after having devoured great multitudes of people, swallowed the king and disappeared. They tell us that King Arthur was not born like other mortals, but was the result of a magical contrivance; that he had great luck in killing giants; that he killed one in France that had the cheerful habit of eating some thirty men a day. That this giant had clothes woven of the beards of the kings he had devoured. To cap the climax, one of the authors of this book was promoted for having written the only reliable history of his country.

In all the histories of those days there is hardly a single truth. Facts were considered unworthy of preservation. Anything that really happened was not of sufficient interest or importance to be recorded. The great religious historian, Eusebius, ingenuously remarks that in his history he carefully omitted whatever tended to discredit the church, and that he piously magnified all that conduced to her glory.

The same glorious principle was scrupulously adhered to by all the historians of that time.

They wrote, and the people believed, that the tracks of Pharoah's chariots were still visible on the sands of the Red Sea, and that they had been miraculously preserved from the winds and waves as perpetual witnesses of the great miracle there performed.

It is safe to say that every truth in the histories of those times is the result of accident or mistake.

They accounted for everything as the work of good and evil spirits. With cause and effect they had nothing to do. Facts were in no way related to each other. God, governed by infinite caprice, filled the world with miracles and disconnected events. From the quiver of his hatred came the arrows of famine, pestilence, and death.

The moment that the idea is abandoned that all is natural, that all phenomena are the necessary links in the endless chain of being, the conception of history becomes impossible. With the ghosts, the present is not the child of the past, nor the mother of the future. In the domain of religion all is chance, accident, and caprice.

Do not forget, I pray you, that our creeds were written by the contemporaries of these historians.

The same idea was applied to law. It was believed by our intelligent ancestors that all law derived its sacredness and its binding force from the fact that it had been communicated to man by the ghosts. Of course it was not pretended that the ghosts told everybody the law; but they told it to a few, and the few told it to the people, and the people, as a rule, paid them exceedingly well for their trouble. It was thousands of ages before the people commenced making laws for themselves, and strange as it may appear, most of these laws were vastly superior to the ghost article.

Through the web and woof of human legislation began to run and shine and glitter the golden thread of justice.

During these years of darkness it was believed that rather than see an act of injustice done; rather than see the innocent suffer; rather than see the guilty triumph, some ghost would interfere. This belief, as a rule, gave great satisfaction to the victorious party, and as the other man was dead, no complaint was heard from him.

This doctrine was the sanctification of brute force and chance. They had trials by battle, by fire, by water, and by lot. Persons were made to grasp hot iron, and if it burned them their guilt was established. Others, with tied hands and feet, were cast into the sea, and if they sank, the verdict of guilty was unanimous,—if they did not sink, they were in league with devils.

So in England, persons charged with crime could appeal to the corsned. The corsned was a piece of the sacramental bread. If the defendant could swallow this piece he went acquit. Godwin, Earl of Kent, in the time of Edward the Confessor, appealed to the corsned. He failed to swallow it and was choked to death.

The ghosts and their followers always took delight in torture, in cruel and unusual punishments. For the infraction of most of their laws, death was the penalty—death produced by stoning and by fire. Sometimes, when man committed only murder, he was allowed to flee to some city of refuge. Murder was a crime against man. But for saying certain words, or denying certain doctrines, or for picking up sticks on certain days, or for worshiping the wrong ghost, or for failing to pray to the right one, or for laughing at a priest, or for saying that wine was not blood, or that bread was not flesh, or for failing to regard ram's horns as artillery, or for insisting that a dry bone was scarcely sufficient to take the place of water works, or that a raven, as a rule, made a poor landlord:—death, produced by all the ways that the ingenuity of hatred could devise, was the penalty.

Law is a growth—it is a science. Right and wrong exist in the nature of things. Things are not right because they are commanded, nor wrong because they are prohibited. There are real crimes enough without creating artificial ones. All progress in legislation has for centuries consisted in repealing the laws of the ghosts.

The idea of right and wrong is born of man's capacity to enjoy and suffer. If man could not suffer, if he could not inflict injury upon his fellow, if he could neither feel nor inflict pain, the idea of right and wrong never would have entered his brain. But for this, the word conscience never would have passed the lips of man.

There is one good—happiness. There is but one sin—selfishness. All law should be for the preservation of the one and the destruction of the other.

Under the regime of the ghosts, laws were not supposed to exist in the nature of things. They were supposed to be simply the irresponsible command of a ghost. These commands were not supposed to rest upon reason, they were the product of arbitrary will.

The penalties for the violation of these laws were as cruel as the laws were senseless and absurd. Working on the Sabbath and murder were both punished with death. The tendency of such laws is to blot from the human heart the sense of justice.

To show you how perfectly every department of knowledge, or ignorance rather, was saturated with superstition, I will for a moment refer to the science of language.

It was thought by our fathers that Hebrew was the original language; that it was taught to Adam in the Garden of Eden by the Almighty; and that consequently all languages came from, and could be traced to, the Hebrew. Every fact inconsistent with that idea was discarded. According to the ghosts, the trouble at the tower of Babel accounted for the fact that all people did not speak Hebrew. The Babel business settled all questions in the science of language.

After a time, so many facts were found to be inconsistent with the Hebrew idea that it began to fall into disrepute, and other languages began to compete for the honor of being the original.

Andre Kempe, in 1569, published a work on the language of Paradise, in which he maintained that God spoke to Adam in Swedish; that Adam answered in Danish; and that the serpent—which appears to me quite probable—spoke to Eve in French. Erro, in a work published at Madrid, took the ground that Basque was the language spoken in the Garden of Eden; but in 1850 Goropius published his celebrated work at Antwerp, in which he put the whole matter at rest by showing, beyond all doubt, that the language spoken in Paradise was neither more nor less than plain Holland Dutch.

The real founder of the science of language was Liebniz, a contemporary of Sir Isaac Newton. He discarded the idea that all languages could be traced to one language. He maintained that language was a natural growth. Experience teaches us that this must be so. Words are continually dying and continually being born. Words are naturally and necessarily produced. Words are the garments of thought, the robes of ideas. Some are as rude as the skins of wild beasts, and others glisten and glitter like silk and gold. They have been born of hatred and revenge, of love and self-sacrifice, of hope and fear, of agony and joy. These words are born of the terror and beauty of nature. The stars have fashioned them. In them mingle the darkness and the dawn. From everything they have taken something. Words are the crystallizations of human history, of all that man has enjoyed and suffered—his victories and defeats—all that he has lost and won. Words are the shadows of all that has been—the mirrors of all that is.

The ghosts also enlightened our fathers in astronomy and geology. According to them the earth was made out of nothing, and a little more nothing having been taken than was used in the construction of this world, the stars were made out of what was left over. Cosmas, in the sixth century, taught that the stars were impelled by angels, who either carried them on their shoulders, rolled them in front of them, or drew them after. He also taught that each angel that pushed a star took great pains to observe what the other angels were doing, so that the relative distances between the stars might always remain the same. He also gave his idea as to the form of the world.

He stated that the world was a vast parallelogram; that on the outside was a strip of land, like the frame of a common slate; that then there was a strip of water, and in the middle a great piece of land; that Adam and Eve lived on the outer strip; that their descendants, with the exception of the Noah family, were drowned by a flood on this outer strip; that the ark finally rested on the middle piece of land where we now are. He accounted for night and day by saying that on the outside strip of land there was a high mountain, around which the sun and moon revolved, and that when the sun was on the other side of the mountain, it was night; and when on this side, it was day.

He also declared that the earth was flat. This he proved by many passages from the Bible. Among other reasons for believing the earth to be flat, he brought forward the following: We are told in the New Testament that Christ shall come again in glory and power, and all the world shall see him. Now, if the world is round, how are the people on the other side going to see Christ when he comes? That settled the question, and the church not only endorsed the book, but declared that whoever believed less or more than stated by Cosmas was a heretic.

In those blessed days, Ignorance was a king and Science an outcast.

They knew the moment this earth ceased to be the center of the universe, and became a mere speck in the starry heaven of existence, that their religion would become a childish fable of the past.

In the name and by the authority of the ghosts, men enslaved their fellowmen; they trampled upon the rights of women and children. In the name and by the authority of ghosts, they bought and sold and destroyed each other; they filled heaven with tyrants and earth with slaves, the present with despair and the future with horror. In the name and by the authority of the ghosts, they imprisoned the human mind, polluted the conscience, hardened the heart, subverted justice, crowned robbery, sainted hypocrisy, and extinguished for a thousand years the torch of reason.

I have endeavored, in some faint degree, to show you what has happened, and what always will happen when men are governed by superstition and fear; when they desert the sublime standard of reason; when they take the words of others and do not investigate for themselves.

Even the great men of those days were nearly as weak in this matter as the most ignorant. Kepler, one of the greatest men of the world, an astronomer second to none, although he plucked from the stars the secrets of the universe, was an astrologer, and really believed that he could predict the career of a man by finding what star was in the ascendant at his birth. This great man breathed, so to speak, the atmosphere of this time. He believed in the music of spheres, and assigned alto, bass, tenor, and treble to certain stars.

Tycho Brahe, another astronomer, kept an idiot, whose disconnected and meaningless words he carefully set down, and then put them together in such manner as to make prophecies, and then waited patiently to see them fulfilled. Luther believed that he had actually seen the devil, and had discussed points of theology with him. The human mind was in chains. Every idea almost was a monster. Thought was deformed. Facts were looked upon as worthless. Only the wonderful was worth preserving. Things that actually happened were not considered worth recording;—real occurrences were too common. Everybody expected the miraculous.

The ghosts were supposed to be busy; devils were thought to be the most industrious things in the universe, and with these imps, every occurrence of an unusual character was in some way connected. There was no order, no serenity, no certainty in anything. Everything depended upon ghosts and phantoms. Man was, for the most part, at the mercy of malevolent spirits. He protected himself as best he could with holy water and tapers and wafers and cathedrals. He made noises and rang bells to frighten the ghosts, and he made music to charm them. He used smoke to choke them, and incense to please them. He wore beads and crosses. He said prayers, and hired others to say them. He fasted when he was hungry, and feasted when he was not. He believed everything that seemed unreasonable, just to appease the ghosts. He humbled himself. He crawled in the dust. He shut the doors and windows, and excluded every ray of light from the temple of the soul. He debauched and polluted his own mind, and toiled night and day to repair the walls of his own prison. From the garden of his heart he plucked and trampled upon the holy flowers of pity.

The priest reveled in horrible descriptions of hell. Concerning the wrath of God, they grew eloquent. They denounced man as totally depraved. They made reason blasphemy, and pity a crime. Nothing so delighted them as painting the torments and sufferings of the lost. Over the worm that never dies they grew poetic; and the second death filled them with a kind of holy delight. According to them, the smoke and cries ascending from hell were the perfume and music of heaven.

At the risk of being tiresome, I have said what I have to show you the productions of the human mind, when enslaved; the effects of widespread ignorance—the results of fear. I want to convince you that every form of slavery is a viper, that, sooner or later, will strike its poison fangs into the bosoms of men.

The first great step towards progress, is for man to cease to be the slave of man; the second, to cease to be the slave of the monsters of his own creation—of the ghosts and phantoms of the air.

For ages the human race was imprisoned. Through the bars and grates came a few struggling rays of light. Against these grates and bars Science pressed its pale and thoughtful face, wooed by the holy dawn of human advancement.

Men found that the real was the useful; that what a man knows is better than what a ghost says; that an event is more valuable than a prophecy. They found that diseases were not produced by spirits, and could not be cured by frightening them away. They found that death was as natural as life. They began to study the anatomy and chemistry of the human body, and found that all was natural and within the domain of law.

The conjurer and sorcerer were discarded, and the physician and surgeon employed. They found that the earth was not flat, that the stars were not mere specks. They found that being born under a particular planet had nothing to do with the fortunes of men.

The astrologer was discharged and the astronomer took his place.

They found that the earth had swept through the constellations for millions of ages. They found that good and evil were produced by natural causes, and not by ghosts; that man could not be good enough or bad enough to stop or cause a rain; that diseases were produced as naturally as grass, and were not sent as punishments upon man for failing to believe a certain creed. They found that man, through intelligence, could take advantage of the forces of nature—that he could make the waves, the winds, the flames, and the lightnings of heaven do his bidding and minister to his wants. They found that the ghosts knew nothing of benefit to man; that they were utterly ignorant of geology—of astronomy— of geography;—that they knew nothing of history;—that they were poor doctors and worse surgeons;—that they knew nothing of law and less of justice; that they were without brains, and utterly destitute of hearts; that they knew nothing of the rights of men; that they were despisers of women, the haters of progress, the enemies of science, and the destroyers of liberty.

The condition of the world during the Dark Ages shows exactly the result of enslaving the bodies and souls of men. In those days there was no freedom. Labor was despised, and a laborer was considered but little above a beast. Ignorance, like a vast cowl, covered the brain of the world, and superstition ran riot with the imagination of man. The air was filled with angels, with demons and monsters. Credulity sat upon the throne of the soul, and Reason was an exiled king. A man to be distinguished must be a soldier or a monk. War and theology, that is to say, murder and hypocrisy, were the principal employments of man. Industry was a slave, theft was commerce; murder was war, hypocrisy was religion.

Every Christian country maintained that it was no robbery to take the property of Mohammedans by force, and no murder to kill the owners. Lord Bacon was the first man of note who maintained that a Christian country was bound to keep its plighted faith with an infidel nation. Reading and writing were considered dangerous arts. Every layman who could read and write was suspected of being a heretic. All thought was discouraged. They forged chains of superstition for the minds, and manacles of iron for the bodies of men. The earth was ruled by the cowl and the sword,—by the miter and scepter,—by the altar and throne,—by Fear and Force,—by Ignorance and Faith,—by ghouls and ghosts.

In the fifteenth century the following law was in force in England:

"That whosoever reads the Scriptures in the mother tongue, shall forfeit land, cattle, life, and goods from their heirs forever, and so be condemned for heretics to God, enemies to the crown, and most arrant traitors to the land."

During the first year this law was in force thirty-nine were hanged for its violation and their bodies burned.

In the sixteenth century men were burned because they failed to kneel to a procession of monks.

The slightest word uttered against the superstition of the time was punished with death.

Even the reformers, so-called, of those days, had no idea of intellectual liberty—no idea even of toleration. Luther, Knox, Calvin believed in religious liberty only when they were in the minority. The moment they were clothed with power they began to exterminate with fire and sword.

Castalio was the first minister who advocated the liberty of the soul. He was regarded by the reformers as a criminal, and treated as though he had committed the crime of crimes.

Bodinus, a lawyer of France, about the same time, wrote a few words in favor of the freedom of conscience, but public opinion was overwhelmingly against him. The people were ready, anxious, and willing, with whip, and chain, and fire, to drive from the mind of man the heresy that he had a right to think.

Montaigne, a man blest with so much common sense that he was the most uncommon man of his time, was the first to raise a voice against torture in France. But what was the voice of one man against the terrible cry of ignorant, infatuated, superstitious, and malevolent millions? It was the cry of a drowning man in the wild roar of the cruel sea.

In spite of the efforts of the brave few the infamous war against the freedom of the soul was waged until at least one hundred millions of human beings—fathers, mothers, brothers, sisters— with hopes, loves, and aspirations like ourselves, were sacrificed upon the cruel altar of an ignorant faith. They perished in every way by which death can be produced. Every nerve of pain was sought out and touched by the believers in ghosts.

For my part I glory in the fact that here in the New World,— in the United States,—liberty of conscience was first guaranteed to man, and that the Constitution of the United States was the first great decree entered in the high court of human equity forever divorcing church and state,—the first injunction granted against the interference of the ghosts. This was one of the grandest steps ever taken by the human race in the direction of Progress.

You will ask what has caused this wonderful change in three hundred years. And I answer—the inventions and discoveries of the few;—the brave thoughts, the heroic utterances of the few;— the acquisition of a few facts.

Besides, you must remember that every wrong in some way tends to abolish itself. It is hard to make a lie stand always. A lie will not fit a fact. It will only fit another lie made for the purpose. The life of a lie is simply a question of time. Nothing but truth is immortal. The nobles and kings quarreled;—the priests began to dispute;—the ideas of government began to change.

In 1441 printing was discovered. At that time the past was a vast cemetery with hardly an epitaph. The ideas of man had mostly perished in the brain that produced them. The lips of the human race had been sealed. Printing gave pinions to thought. It preserved ideas. It made it possible for man to bequeath to the future the riches of his brain, the wealth of his soul. At first, it was used to flood the world with the mistakes of the ancients, but since that time it has been flooding the world with light.

When people read they begin to reason, and when they reason they progress. This was another grand step in the direction of Progress.

The discovery of powder, that put the peasant almost upon a par with the prince;—that put an end to the so-called age of chivalry;—that released a vast number of men from the armies;—that gave pluck and nerve a chance with brute strength.

The discovery of America, whose shores were trod by the restless feet of adventure;—that brought people holding every shade of superstition together;—that gave the world an opportunity to compare notes, and to laugh at the follies of each other. Out of this strange mingling of all creeds, and superstitions, and facts, and theories, and countless opinions, came the Great Republic.

Every fact has pushed a superstition from the brain and a ghost from the clouds. Every mechanic art is an educator. Every loom, every reaper and mower, every steamboat, every locomotive, every engine, every press, every telegraph is a missionary of Science and an apostle of Progress. Every mill, every furnace, every building with its wheels and levers, in which something is made for the convenience, for the use, and for the comfort and elevation of man, is a church, and every schoolhouse is a temple.

Education is the most radical thing in the world.

To teach the alphabet is to inaugurate a revolution.

To build a schoolhouse is to construct a fort.

Every library is an arsenal filled with the weapons and ammunition of Progress, and every fact is a monitor with sides of iron and a turret of steel.

I thank the inventors, the discoverers, the thinkers. I thank
Columbus and Magellan. I thank Galileo, and Copernicus, and
Kepler, and Descartes, and Newton, and Laplace. I thank Locke,
and Hume, and Bacon, and Shakespeare, and Kant, and Fichte,
and Leibniz, and Goethe. I thank Fulton, and Watts, and Volta,
and Galvani, and Franklin, and Morse, who made lightning the
messenger of men. I thank Humboldt, the Shakespeare of science.
I thank Crompton and Arkwright, from whose brains leaped the
looms and spindles that clothe the world. I thank Luther for protesting
against the abuses of the church, and I denounce him because he
was the enemy of liberty. I thank Calvin for writing a book in
favor of religious freedom, and I abhor him because he burned
Servetus. I thank Knox for resisting Episcopal persecution, and I
hate him because he persecuted in his turn. I thank the Puritans
for saying "Resistance to tyrants is obedience to God," and yet I
am compelled to say that they were tyrants themselves. I thank
Thomas Paine because he was a believer in liberty, and because
he did as much to make my country free as any other human
being. I thank Voltaire, that great man who, for half a century,
was the intellectual emperor of Europe, and who, from his throne
at the foot of the Alps, pointed the finger of scorn at every hypocrite
in Christendom. I thank Darwin, Haeckel and Büchner, Spencer,
Tyndall and Huxley, Draper, Lecky and Buckle.

I thank the inventors, the discoverers, the thinkers, the scientists, the explorers. I thank the honest millions who have toiled.

I thank the brave men with brave thoughts. They are the Atlases
upon whose broad and mighty shoulders rest the grand fabric of
civilization. They are the men who have broken, and are still breaking,
the chains of Superstition. They are the Titans who carried Olympus
by assault, and who will soon stand victors upon Sinai's crags.

We are beginning to learn that to exchange a mistake for the
truth—a superstition for a fact—to ascertain the real—is to progress.

Happiness is the only possible good, and all that tends to
the happiness of man is right, and is of value. All that tends
to develop the bodies and minds of men; all that gives us better

houses, better clothes, better food, better pictures, grander music, better heads, better hearts; all that renders us more intellectual and more loving, nearer just; that makes us better husbands and wives, better children, better citizens—all these things combine to produce what I call Progress.

Man advances only as he overcomes the obstructions of Nature, and this can be done only by labor and by thought. Labor is the foundation of all. Without labor, and without great labor, progress is impossible. The progress of the world depends upon the men who walk in the fresh furrows and through the rustling corn; upon those who sow and reap; upon those whose faces are radiant with the glare of furnace fires; upon the delvers in the mines, and the workers in shops; upon those who give to the winter air the ringing music of the axe; upon those who battle with the boisterous billows of the sea; upon the inventors and discoverers; upon the brave thinkers.

From the surplus produced by labor, schools and universities are built and fostered. From this surplus the painter is paid for the productions of the pencil; the sculptor for chiseling shapeless rock into forms divinely beautiful; and the poet for singing the hopes, the loves, the memories, and the aspirations of the world. This surplus has given us the books in which we converse with the dead and living kings of the human race. It has given us all there is of beauty, of elegance, and of refined happiness.

I am aware that there is a vast difference of opinion as to what progress really is; that many denounce the ideas of today as destructive of all happiness—of all good. I know that there are many worshipers of the past. They venerate the ancient because it is ancient. They see no beauty in anything from which they do not blow the dust of ages with the breath of praise. They say, no masters like the old; no religion, no governments like the ancient; no orators, no poets, no statesmen like those who have been dust for two thousand years. Others love the modern simply because it is modern.

We should have gratitude enough to acknowledge the obligations we are under to the great and heroic of antiquity, and independence enough not to believe what they said simply because they said it.

With the idea that labor is the basis of progress goes the truth that labor must be free. The laborer must be a free man.

The free man, working for wife and child, gets his head and hands in partnership.

To do the greatest amount of work in the shortest space of time is the problem of free labor.

Slavery does the least work in the longest space of time.

Free labor will give us wealth. Free thought will give us truth.

Slowly but surely man is freeing his imagination of these sexless phantoms, of these cruel ghosts. Slowly but surely he is rising above the superstitions of the past. He is learning to rely upon himself. He is beginning to find that labor is the only prayer that ought to be answered, and that hoping, toiling, aspiring, suffering men and women are of more importance than all the ghosts that ever wandered through the fenceless fields of space.

The believers in ghosts claim still that they are the only wise and virtuous people upon the earth; claim still that there is a difference between them and unbelievers so vast, that they will be infinitely rewarded, and the others infinitely punished.

I ask you, do the theories and doctrines of the theologians satisfy the heart or the brain of the nineteenth century?

Have the churches the confidence of mankind?

Does the merchant give credit to a man because he belongs to a church?

Does the banker loan money to a man because he is a Methodist or a Baptist?

Will a certificate of good standing in any church be taken as collateral security for one dollar?

Will you take the word of a church member, or his note, or his oath, simply because he is a church member?

Are the clergy, as a class, better, kinder, and more generous to their families—to their fellowmen—than doctors, lawyers, merchants, and farmers?

Does a belief in ghosts and unreasonable things necessarily make people honest?

When a man loses confidence in Moses, must the people lose confidence in him?

Does not the credit system in morals breed extravagance in sin?

Why send missionaries to other lands while every penitentiary in ours is filled with criminals?

Is it philosophical to say that they who do right carry a cross?

Is it a source of joy to think that perdition is the destination of nearly all of the children of men?

Is it worthwhile to quarrel about original sin—when there is so much copy?

Does it pay to dispute about baptism, and the Trinity, and predestination, and apostolic succession and the infallibility of churches, of popes, and of books? Does all this do any good?

Are the theologians welcomers of new truths? Are they noted for their candor? Do they treat an opponent with common fairness? Are they investigators? Do they pull forward, or do they hold back?

Is science indebted to the church for a solitary fact?

What church is an asylum for a persecuted truth?

What great reform has been inaugurated by the church?

Did the church abolish slavery?

Has the church raised its voice against war?

I used to think that there was in religion no real restraining force. Upon this point my mind has changed. Religion will prevent man from committing artificial crimes and offenses.

A man committed murder. The evidence was so conclusive that he confessed his guilt.

He was asked why he killed his fellowman.

He replied: "For money."

"Did you get any?"

"Yes."

"How much?"

Fifteen cents."

"What did you do with this money?"

"Spent it."

"What for?"

"Liquor."

"What else did you find upon the dead man?"

"He had his dinner in a bucket—some meat and bread."

"What did you do with that?"

"I ate the bread."

"What did you do with the meat?"

"I threw it away."

"Why?"

"It was Friday."

Just to the extent that man has freed himself from the dominion of ghosts he has advanced. Just to the extent that he has freed himself from the tyrants of his own creation he has progressed. Just to the extent that he has investigated for himself he has lost confidence in superstition.

With knowledge obedience becomes intelligent acquiescence— it is no longer degrading. Acquiescence in the understood—in the known—is the act of a sovereign, not of a slave. It ennobles, it does not degrade.

Man has found that he must give liberty to others in order to have it himself. He has found that a master is also a slave;— that a tyrant is himself a serf. He has found that governments should be founded and administered by man and for man; that the rights of all are equal; that the powers that be are not ordained by God; that woman is at least the equal of man; that men existed before books; that religion is one of the phases of thought through which the world is passing; that all creeds were made by man; that everything is natural; that a miracle is an impossibility; that we know nothing of origin and destiny; that concerning the unknown we are all equally ignorant; that the pew has the right to contradict what the pulpit asserts; that man is responsible only to himself and those he injures; and that all have a right to think.

True religion must be free. Without perfect liberty of mind there can be no true religion. Without liberty the brain is a dungeon—the mind a convict. The slave may bow and cringe and crawl, but he cannot adore—he cannot love.

True religion is the perfume of a free and grateful heart. True religion is a subordination of the passions to the perceptions of the intellect. True religion is not a theory—it is a practice. It is not a creed—it is a life.

A theory that is afraid of investigation is undeserving a place in the human mind.

I do not pretend to tell what all the truth is. I do not pretend to have fathomed the abyss, nor to have floated on outstretched wings level with the dim heights of thought. I simply plead for freedom. I denounce the cruelties and horrors of slavery. I ask for light and air for the souls of men. I say, take off those chains— break those manacles—free those limbs—release that brain! I plead for the right to think—to reason—to investigate. I ask that the future may be enriched with the honest thoughts of men. I implore every human being to be a soldier in the army of progress.

I will not invade the rights of others. You have no right to erect your tollgate upon the highways of thought. You have no right to leap from the hedges of superstition and strike down the pioneers of the human race. You have no right to sacrifice the liberties of man upon the altars of ghosts. Believe what you may; preach what you desire; have all the forms and ceremonies you please; exercise your liberty in your own way but extend to all others the same right.

I will not attack your doctrines nor your creeds if they accord liberty to me. If they hold thought to be dangerous—if they aver that doubt is a crime, then I attack them one and all, because they enslave the minds of men.

I attack the monsters, the phantoms of imagination that have ruled the world. I attack slavery. I ask for room—room for the human mind.

Why should we sacrifice a real world that we have, for one we know not of? Why should we enslave ourselves? Why should we forge fetters for our own hands? Why should we be the slaves of phantoms? The darkness of barbarism was the womb of these shadows. In the light of science they cannot cloud the sky forever. They have reddened the hands of man with innocent blood. They made the cradle a curse, and the grave a place of torment.

They blinded the eyes and stopped the ears of the human race. They subverted all ideas of justice by promising infinite rewards for finite virtues, and threatening infinite punishment for finite offenses.

They filled the future with heavens and with hells, with the shining peaks of selfish joy and the lurid abysses of flame. For ages they kept the world in ignorance and awe, in want and misery, in fear and chains.

I plead for light, for air, for opportunity. I plead for individual independence. I plead for the rights of labor and of thought. I plead for a chainless future. Let the ghosts go—justice remains. Let them disappear—men and women and children are left. Let the monsters fade away—the world is here with its hills and seas and plains, with its seasons of smiles and frowns, its spring of leaf and bud, its summer of shade and flower and murmuring stream; its autumn with the laden boughs, when the withered banners of the corn are still, and gathered fields are growing strangely wan; while death, poetic death, with hands that color what they touch, weaves in the Autumn wood her tapestries of gold and brown.

The world remains with its winters and homes and firesides, where grow and bloom the virtues of our race. All these are left; and music, with its sad and thrilling voice, and all there is of art and song and hope and love and aspiration high. All these remain. Let the ghosts go—we will worship them no more.

Man is greater than these phantoms. Humanity is grander

than all the creeds, than all the books. Humanity is the great sea, and these creeds, and books, and religions, are but the waves of a day. Humanity is the sky, and these religions and dogmas and theories are but the mists and clouds changing continually, destined finally to melt away.

That which is founded upon slavery, and fear, and ignorance cannot endure. In the religion of the future there will be men and women and children, all the aspirations of the soul, and all the tender humanities of the heart.

Let the ghosts go. We will worship them no more. Let them cover their eyeless sockets with their fleshless hands and fade forever from the imaginations of men.